THE WORKS

KEY STAGE 1

Pie Corbett – poet, storyteller and educator – was a primary teacher and head teacher. He worked in teacher training and was English inspector in Gloucestershire. He advised the English National Literacy Strategy on teaching poetry, writing and grammar. Author and editor of over 250 books, he was made a Doctor of Letters in 2009 by the University of Winchester for services to poetry, storytelling and creative education. Pie works across the country running research and development projects with schools.

THE
WORKS

KEY STAGE 1

POEMS AND RHYMES TO
ENJOY, READ, PERFORM
AND LEARN BY HEART

Chosen
by
PIE CORBETT

MACMILLAN CHILDREN'S BOOKS

*This book is dedicated to Mum and Dad, who
introduced us to the world of poems and stories which
are bright beacons when the night grows dark*

First published 2006 by Macmillan Children's Books

This edition published 2014 by Macmillan Children's Books
a division of Macmillan Publishers Limited
20 New Wharf Road, London N1 9RR
Basingstoke and Oxford
Associated companies throughout the world
www.panmacmillan.com

ISBN 978-1-4472-7484-1

Contents

Nursery Rhymes

Contents

Circle Songs

Contents

Action Rhymes and Songs

Contents

Dipping, Skipping and Clapping

Contents

Counting Rhymes

Tongue-twisters

Contents

Riddle Me Ree

Adventures with Pirates, Ghosts and Aliens

Contents

Fairies, Princesses and Mermaids

Contents

My Feelings and I

Contents

The Animal World

Contents

Families and Other Folk

Contents

Natural World – Day Turning, Seasons Changing

Contents

A Saying from Zimbabwe

If you can walk
You can dance
If you can talk
You can sing

Anon.

Introduction

This anthology brings together poems, rhymes and songs that a teacher might need when working in nursery, preschool settings and at Key Stage 1. Babies play with language, repeating sounds and taking delight in making rhythmic noises. Toddlers repeat new and invented words and phrases, often in a sing-song voice, ritualizing the routine as they play. This collection builds upon these early foundations.

The poems are arranged so that the collection starts with a bank of common nursery rhymes. Recent research and the experience of many reception teachers suggests that the majority of children entering schools are familiar with only a handful of such rhymes. Learning a rhyme a week, during the Early Years and Key Stage 1, would provide an impressive bank of some ninety rhymes and poems – imagine that, a rich repertoire of musical words, images, rhythms and movement – so children continue playing with language for its own sake as well as making memorable patterns. It seems unthinkable that children might slip through our hands without ever having experienced the joy of 'Inky pinky ponky . . .' or taking part in 'The Farmer's in His Den'.

Building up a bank of well-loved rhymes, songs and poems is an important part of early literacy development . . . as well as a source of great joy. It influences a positive start in reading and writing and also adds to the living library of stories and images that lie at the heart of our world culture.

The traditional nursery rhymes are followed by banks of action and counting rhymes, singing games, clapping, skipping and dipping rhymes as well as circle songs. The poems vary from classics such as 'The Owl and the Pussy-cat', which flows with such rhythmic and memorable language that it should be held in the heart of every child, through to more modern poems. Many poems provide simple patterns that children might use for their own writing. Some are perfect for performance, while others savour language and linger over experience, bringing the world alive. Some may be responded to by role play, making models, painting, storytelling or music making.

Most of these poems are suitable for solo or group performances and will become part of a child's poetic repertoire. Poems cannot always be easily 'understood'. However, in great poems, the music and meaning of the words, rhythms and images resonate in the memory. Draw simple 'poetry maps' to help children remember the lines and use actions to support performance. Vary volume, pace and expression to emphasize meaning. Music, singing, dance, drama and art may also be used to make the poems memorable experiences rather then just words upon a page. Through rereading, savouring and performance, many of these poems will become favourites that children take to heart for the rest of their lives.

I have included in the index a suggested breakdown of poems into different years in case a school wishes to organize their poetry in this way, with the more demanding poems left for Year 2. Of course, children love to revisit old favourites in the same way that I still find myself playing the Beatles' songs forty years after I first heard them. There is a common human need to listen to and join in with basic rhythmic patterns. For what is common to every culture across the world? It is the songs and poems, the stories, dances, music, religion and art that lie at the heart of all cultures. If these aspects of the curriculum do not lie at the heart of our schools, then we run the risk of having schools with no heart, no soul and the human spirit undernourished. If our children's education does not allow children to create and bring into being poems and songs, then our education is just dry dust upon the wind . . . for the opposite of creation is destruction.

The poems and rhymes are here to surprise, to challenge, to delight, to create wonder as well as the inexplicable charm of rhythmic and memorable language. There are poems that preserve and celebrate experience, both real and imagined; poems that will act as a catalyst to children's own writing; poems that ring true; poems that help explain the world to ourselves and, through reading, help us find our own place in the world; poems that will act as deep grooves in the memory; poems that will act as lights in the darkness, and poems that touch our common genius.

Pie Corbett

At the back you will find indexes showing:

- a glossary of poetic terms;
- an alphabet of advice for young poetry writers;
- an alphabet of poetry-reading ideas;
- notes on how to perform some of the rhymes;
- the poems organized by year group and type.

Nursery Rhymes

Each Peach Pear Plum

Each peach pear plum
I spy Tom Thumb.

Tom Thumb fast asleep
I spy Bo-Peep.

Bo-Beep round the corner
I spy Jack Horner.

Jack Horner up a pole
I spy King Cole.

King Cole drinking juice
I spy Mother Goose.

Mother Goose told a story
I spy Jackanory.

Anon.

Three Blind Mice

Three blind mice, three blind mice,
See how they run, see how they run!
They all ran after the farmer's wife,
Who cut off their tails with a carving knife,
Did you ever see such a thing in your life,
As three blind mice?

Anon.

Hickory, Dickory, Dock

Hickory, dickory, dock,
The mouse ran up the clock.
The clock struck one,
The mouse ran down,
Hickory, dickory, dock.

Anon.

Baa, Baa, Black Sheep

Baa, baa, black sheep,
Have you any wool?
Yes, sir, yes, sir,
Three bags full;
One for the master,
And one for the dame,
And one for the little boy
Who lives down the lane.

Anon.

Little Boy Blue

Little Boy Blue, come blow your horn,
The sheep's in the meadow, the cow's in the corn.
Where's the boy that looks after the sheep?
He's under a haycock fast asleep.
Dare you wake him? No, not I!
For if I do, he's sure to cry.

Anon.

Little Jack Horner

Little Jack Horner
Sat in the corner,
Eating a Christmas pie;
He put in his thumb,
And pulled out a plum,
And said, 'What a good boy am I!'

Anon.

Little Miss Muffet

Little Miss Muffet
Sat on a tuffet,
Eating her curds and whey;
Along came a spider,
That sat down beside her
And frightened Miss Muffet away.

Anon.

Hey Diddle Diddle

Hey diddle diddle,
The cat and the fiddle,
The cow jumped over the moon;
The little dog laughed
To see such fun,
And the dish ran away with the spoon.

Anon.

Rub-a-dub-dub

Rub-a-dub-dub,
Three men in a tub;
And who do you think they be?
The butcher, the baker,
The candlestick-maker;
Turn 'em out, knaves all three!

Anon.

Doctor Foster

Doctor Foster went to Gloucester
In a shower of rain;
He stepped in a puddle,
Right up to his middle,
And never went there again,

Anon.

Old Mother Hubbard

Old Mother Hubbard went to the cupboard
To fetch her poor doggie a bone.
But when she got there, the cupboard was bare,
And so the poor doggie had none.

Anon.

Deedle Deedle Dumpling

Deedle deedle dumpling, my son John
Ate a pasty five feet long;
He bit it once, he bit it twice,
Oh, my goodness, it was full of mice!

Anon.

Jack Sprat

Jack Sprat could eat no fat,
    His wife could eat no lean;
And so between them both, you see,
    They licked the platter clean.

Anon.

The North Wind Doth Blow

The north wind doth blow,
  And we shall have snow,
And what will poor robin do then, poor thing?
  He'll sit in a barn,
  And keep himself warm,
  And hide his head under his wing, poor thing.

Anon.

Pat-a-cake

Pat-a-cake, pat-a-cake, baker's man,
Bake me a cake as fast as you can;
Pat it and prick it, and mark it with B,
And put it in the oven for Baby and me.

Anon.

Polly and Sukey

Polly put the kettle on,
Polly put the kettle on,
Polly put the kettle on,
We'll all have tea.

Sukey take it off again,
Sukey take it off again,
Sukey take it off again,
They've all gone away.

Blow the fire and make the toast,
Put the muffins on to roast,
Who is going to eat the most?
We'll all have tea.

Anon.

Pease Porridge

Pease porridge hot, pease porridge cold,
Pease porridge in the pot, nine days old.
Some like it hot, some like it cold,
Some like it in the pot, nine days old.

Anon.

There Was a Crooked Man

There was a crooked man,
And he walked a crooked mile,
And found a crooked sixpence
Against a crooked stile;
He bought a crooked cat,
Which caught a crooked mouse,
And they all lived together
In a little crooked house.

Anon.

Sing a Song of Sixpence

Sing a song of sixpence,
A pocket full of rye;
Four and twenty blackbirds,
Baked in a pie.

When the pie was opened,
The birds began to sing;
Wasn't that a dainty dish,
To set before the king?

The king was in his counting-house,
    Counting out his money;
The queen was in the parlour,
    Eating bread and honey.

The maid was in the garden,
    Hanging out the clothes.
When down came a blackbird,
    And pecked off her nose.

As it fell upon the ground,
    'Twas spied by Jenny Wren,
Who took a stick of sealing wax
    And stuck it on again.

Anon.

Hush Little Baby

Hush little baby, don't say a word,
Papa's going to buy you a mocking bird.

And if that mocking bird won't sing,
Papa's going to buy you a diamond ring.

And if that diamond ring turns to brass,
Papa's going to buy you a looking glass.

And if that looking glass gets broke,
Papa's going to buy you a billy-goat.

And if that billy-goat should run away,
Papa's going to buy you another today.

Anon.

I Had a Little Nut Tree

I had a little nut tree;
Nothing would it bear
But a silver nutmeg
And a golden pear;
The King of Spain's daughter
Came to visit me,
And all for the sake of
My little nut tree.
I skipped over water,
I danced over sea,
And all the birds in the air
Couldn't catch me.

Anon.

Old King Cole

Old King Cole was a merry old soul,
And a merry old soul was he;
He called for his pipe
In the middle of the night
And he called for his fiddlers three.

Each fiddler he had a fiddle,
And the fiddles went tweedle-dee;
Oh, there's none so rare as can compare
With King Cole and his fiddlers three.

Anon.

Jack and Jill

Jack and Jill went up the hill,
   To fetch a pail of water;
Jack fell down and broke his crown,
   And Jill came tumbling after.

Anon.

Circle Songs

The Mulberry Bush

Here we go round the mulberry bush,
The mulberry bush, the mulberry bush;
Here we go round the mulberry bush,
   On a cold and frosty morning.

This is the way we wash our hands,
Wash our hands, wash our hands;
This is the way we wash our hands,
   On a cold and frosty morning.

Here we go round the mulberry bush,
The mulberry bush, the mulberry bush;
Here we go round the mulberry bush,
   On a cold and frosty morning.

This is the way we put on our clothes,
Put on our clothes, put on our clothes;
This is the way we put on our clothes,
   On a cold and frosty morning.

Here we go round the mulberry bush,
The mulberry bush, the mulberry bush;
Here we go round the mulberry bush,
   On a cold and frosty morning.

This is the way we brush our teeth,
Brush our teeth, brush our teeth;
This is the way we brush our teeth,
 On a cold and frosty morning.

Here we go round the mulberry bush,
The mulberry bush, the mulberry bush;
Here we go round the mulberry bush,
 On a cold and frosty morning.

Anon.

Ring-a-ring o' Roses

Ring-a-ring o' roses,
A pocket full of posies.
A-tishoo! A-tishoo!
We all fall down.

Ring-a-ring o' roses,
A pocket full of posies,
One for you, and one for me,
And one for little Moses.
A-tishoo! A-tishoo! We all fall down.

Ring-a-ring o' roses,
A pocket full of posies,
Hush-a, hush-a, we all fall down.
The cows are in the meadow,
Lying fast asleep,
Hush-a, hush-a, we all jump up.

Anon.

Down in the Valley

Down in the valley
  Where the green grass grows,
There stands *Daisy*,
  Washing out her clothes.
She sang and she sang
  And she sang so sweet,
She sang for her playmate
  Across the street.

Playmate, playmate.
  Will you come to tea?
Come next Saturday
  At half past three.
Tea, cakes, pancakes,
  All for you and me.
Won't we have a lovely time
  At half past three.

Anon.

The Farmer's in His Den

The farmer's in his den,
The farmer's in his den,
E I, Adio
The farmer's in his den.

The farmer wants a wife,
The farmer wants a wife,
E I, Adio
The farmer wants a wife.

The wife wants a child,
The wife wants a child,
E I, Adio
The wife wants a child.

The child wants a nurse,
The child wants a nurse,
E I, Adio
The child wants a nurse.

The nurse wants a dog,
The nurse wants a dog,
E I, Adio
The nurse wants a dog.

The dog wants a bone,
The dog wants a bone,
E I, Adio
The dog wants a bone.

We all pat the bone,
We all pat the bone,
E I, Adio
We all pat the bone.

Anon.

Oats and Beans and Barley Grow

Oats and beans and barley grow,
Oats and beans and barley grow.
Do you or I or anyone know
How oats and beans and barley grow?

First the farmer sows his seed,
Then he stands and takes his ease,
Stamps his foot, and claps his hand,
And turns around to view the land.

Waiting for a partner,
Waiting for a partner,
Waiting for a partner,
So open the ring and let one in.

Now you're married you must obey,
You must be true to all you say;
You must be kind, you must be good,
And help your wife to chop the wood.
Chop it thin and carry it in,
And kiss your partner in the ring.

Anon.

Rosy Apple

Rosy apple, lemon and a pear,
A bunch of roses she shall wear,
A sword and pistol by her side,
She shall be a bride.
Take her by the lily-white hand,
Lead her across the water.
Blow her a kiss and say goodbye –
For she's the captain's daughter.

Anon.

Let's Go to Kentucky

Let's go to Kentucky
Let's go to the fair,
To see a senorita,
With flowers in her hair.
Shake it, shake it, shake it,
Shake it if you can;
And if you cannot shake it,
Then do the best you can.
Oh, rumble to the bottom,
Rumble to the top,
Round and round,
Round and round,
Until you cannot stop!

Anon.

There Was a Princess Long Ago

There was a princess long ago,
Long ago, long ago,
There was a princess long ago,
Long, long ago.

And she lived in a big high tower,
A big high tower, a big high tower,
And she lived in a big high tower,
Long, long ago.

A wicked fairy waved her wand,
Waved her wand, waved her wand,
A wicked fairy waved her wand,
Long, long ago.

The princess slept for a hundred years,
A hundred years, a hundred years,
The princess slept for a hundred years,
Long, long ago.

A great big forest grew around,
Grew around, grew around,
A great big forest grew around,
Long, long ago.

A gallant prince came riding by,
Riding by, riding by,
A gallant prince came riding by,
Long, long ago.

He chopped the trees down one by one,
One by one, one by one,
He chopped the trees down one by one,
Long, long ago.

He took the princess by the hand,
By the hand, by the hand,
He took the princess by the hand,
Long, long ago.

So everybody's happy now,
Happy now, happy now,
So everybody's happy now,
Happy now.

Anon.

Poor Jenny

Poor Jenny is a-weeping,
A-weeping, a-weeping,
Poor Jenny is a-weeping,
On a bright summer's day.

Oh, why are you weeping,
A-weeping, a-weeping,
Why are you weeping,
On a bright summer's day?

I'm weeping for a loved one,
A loved one, a loved one,
I'm weeping for a loved one,
On a bright summer's day.

Stand up and choose your loved one,
Your loved one, your loved one,
Stand up and choose your loved one,
On a bright summer's day.

Shake hands before you leave her,
You leave her, you leave her,
Shake hands before you leave her,
On a bright summer's day.

Anon.

Brown Girl in the Ring

Brown girl in the ring,
Tra la la la la,
There's a brown girl in the ring,
Tra la la la la,
There's a brown girl in the ring,
Tra la la la la,
For she like sugar and I like plum.

Then you skip across the ocean,
Tra la la la la,
Then you skip across the ocean,
Tra la la la la,
Then you skip across the ocean,
Tra la la la la,
For she like sugar and I like plum.

Then you show me your motion,
Tra la la la la,
Then you show me your motion,
Tra la la la la,
Then you show me your motion,
Tra la la la la,
For she like sugar and I like plum.

Then you wheel and take your partner,
Tra la la la la,
Then you wheel and take your partner,
Tra la la la la,
Then you wheel and take your partner,
Tra la la la la,
For she like sugar and I like plum.

Anon.

Banyan Tree

Moonshine tonight, come mek we dance an sing,
Moonshine tonight, come mek we dance an sing.
Me deh rock so, yu deh rock so, under banyan tree,
Me deh rock so, yu deh rock so, under banyan tree.

Ladies mek curtsy, an gentlemen mek bow,
Ladies mek curtsy, an gentlemen mek bow.
Me deh rock so, yu deh rock so, under banyan tree,
Me deh rock so, yu deh rock so, under banyan tree.

Den we join hans and dance aroun an roun,
Den we join hans and dance aroun an roun.
Me deh rock so, yu deh rock so, under banyan tree,
Me deh rock so, yu deh rock so, under banyan tree.

Anon.

Do You Know the Muffin Man?

Do you know the muffin man,
  The muffin man, the muffin man,
Do you know the muffin man
  Who lives down Drury Lane?

Yes, I know the muffin man,
  The muffin man, the muffin man,
Yes, I know the muffin man
  Who lives down Drury Lane.

Anon.

Pop Goes the Weasel!

Up and down the City Road,
  In and out the Eagle,
That's the way the money goes,
  Pop goes the weasel!

A ha'penny for a cotton ball,
  A farthing for a needle,
That's the way the money goes,
  Pop goes the weasel!

Half a pound of tuppenny rice,
  Half a pound of treacle,
Mix it up and make it nice,
  Pop goes the weasel!

Every time my mother goes out,
  The monkey's on the table,
Cracking nuts and eating spice,
  Pop goes the weasel!

If you want to buy a pig,
  Buy a pig with hairs on,
Every hair a penny a pair,
  Pop goes the weasel!

Anon.

Nuts in May

Here we go gathering nuts in May,
  Nuts in May, nuts in May,
Here we go gathering nuts in May,
  On a cold and frosty morning.

29

Who will you have for nuts in May,
Nuts in May, nuts in May,
Who will you have for nuts in May,
On a cold and frosty morning?

We'll have *Sasha* for nuts in May,
Nuts in May, nuts in May,
We'll have Sasha for nuts in May,
On a cold and frosty morning.

Who will you have to pull her away,
Pull her away, pull her away,
Who will you have to pull her away,
On a cold and frosty morning?

We'll have *Connor* to pull her away,
Pull her away, pull her away.
We'll have Connor to pull her away,
On a cold and frosty morning.

Anon.

In and Out the Windows

In and out the windows,
In and out the windows,
In and out the windows,
As you have done before.

Stand and face your partner,
Stand and face your partner,
Stand and face your partner,
As you have done before.

Follow her/him to London,
Follow her/him to London,
Follow her/him to London,
As you have done before.

Shake hands before you leave her/him,
Shake hands before you leave her/him,
Shake hands before you leave her/him,
As you have done before.

Anon.

Dusty Bluebells

In and out the dusty bluebells,
In and out the dusty bluebells,
In and out the dusty bluebells,
Who shall be my master?

Tippitty tappitty on your shoulder,
Tippitty tappitty on your shoulder,
Tippitty tappitty on your shoulder,
You shall be my master.

Anon.

Lou, Lou, Skip to Me Lou

Lou, lou, skip to me lou,
Lou, lou, skip to me lou,
Lou, lou, skip to me lou,
   Skip to me lou, my darling.

Lost my partner, what shall I do?
Lost my partner, what shall I do?
Lost my partner, what shall I do?
   Skip to me lou, my darling.

I've found another one, just like you,
I've found another one, just like you,
I've found another one, just like you,
   Skip to me lou, my darling.

Anon.

The Big Ship Sails on the Alley, Alley O

The big ship sails on the alley, alley O,
   The alley, alley O, the alley, alley O.
The big ship sails on the alley, alley O,
   On the last day of September,

The Captain said, 'This will never, never do,
   Never never do, never never do.'
The Captain said, 'This will never, never do,'
   On the last day of September.

The big ship sank to the bottom of the sea,
   The bottom of the sea, the bottom of the sea.
The big ship sank to the bottom of the sea,
   On the last day of September.

We all dip our heads in the deep blue sea,
   The deep blue sea, the deep blue sea.
We all dip our heads in the deep blue sea,
   On the last day of September.

Anon.

One Little Elephant

One little elephant went out one day
Upon a spider's web to play;
He had such tremendous fun
He sent for another elephant to come.

Two little elephants went out one day
Upon a spider's web to play;
They had such tremendous fun
They sent for another elephant to come.

Three little elephants went out one day
Upon a spider's web to play;
They had such tremendous fun
They sent for another elephant to come . . .

Anon.

33

The Hokey Cokey

You put your right arm in,
Your right arm out,
Your right arm in,
And you shake it all about.
You do the Hokey Cokey,
And you turn around,
That's what it's all about.

Chorus
Oh, the Hokey, Cokey, Cokey!
Oh, the Hokey, Cokey, Cokey!
Oh, the Hokey, Cokey, Cokey!
Knees bend,
Arms stretch,
Ra! Ra! Ra!

Add more verses, e.g.
You put your left arm in, *etc.*
You put your right leg in, *etc.*
You put your left leg in, *etc.*
You put your whole self in, *etc.*

Anon.

The Grand Old Duke of York

Oh, the grand old Duke of York,
He had ten thousand men.
He marched them up to the top of the hill,
And he marched them down again.
And when they were up, they were up,
And when they were down, they were down,
And when they were only halfway up,
They were neither up nor down.

Anon.

Drunken Sailor

What shall we do with a drunken sailor,
What shall we do with a drunken sailor,
What shall we do with a drunken sailor,
Ear-lie in the morning?

Hoo-ray and up she rises,
Hoo-ray and up she rises,
Hoo-ray and up she rises,
Ear-lie in the morning,

Anon.

How Many Miles to Babylon?

How many miles to Babylon?
Three score miles and ten.
Can I get there by candlelight?
Yes, and back again.
Open your gates as wide as the sky
And let the king and his men pass by.

Anon.

The Bells of London

Oranges and lemons,
Say the bells of St Clement's.
You owe me five farthings,
Say the bells of St Martin's.
When will you pay me?
Say the bells of Old Bailey.
When I grow rich,
Say the bells of Shoreditch.
When will that be?
Say the bells of Stepney.
I'm sure I don't know,
Says the Great Bell of Bow.

Anon.

The Bells of Northampton

Roast beef and marshmallows,
Say the bells of All Hallows'.
Pancakes and fritters,
Say the bells of St Peter's.
Roast beef and boil'd,
Say the bells of St Giles'.
Poker and tongs,
Say the bells of St John's.

Anon.

London Bridge Is Falling Down

London Bridge is falling down,
  Falling down, falling down,
London Bridge is falling down,
  My fair lady.

Build it up with sticks and stones,
  Sticks and stones, sticks and stones,
Build it up with sticks and stones,
  My fair lady.

Sticks and stones will wear away,
  Wear away, wear away,
Sticks and stones will wear away,
  My fair lady.

Build it up with iron and steel,
   Iron and steel, iron and steel,
Build it up with iron and steel,
   My fair lady.

Iron and steel will rust away,
   Rust away, rust away,
Iron and steel will rust away,
   My fair lady.

Build it up with bricks and clay,
   Bricks and clay, bricks and clay,
Build it up with bricks and clay,
   My fair lady.

Bricks and clay will wash away,
   Wash away, wash away,
Bricks and clay will wash away,
   My fair lady.

Build it up with silver and gold,
   Silver and gold, silver and gold,
Build it up with silver and gold,
   My fair lady.

Silver and gold is stole away,
   Stole away, stole away,
Silver and gold is stole away,
   My fair lady.

Anon.

Action Rhymes and Songs

Peter Works with One Hammer

Peter works with one hammer,
One hammer, one hammer,
Peter works with one hammer,
All day long.

Extra verses
Peter works with two hammers, *etc.*
Peter works with three hammers, *etc.*
Peter works with four hammers, *etc.*
Peter works with five hammers, *etc.*

Anon.

I'm a Little Teapot

I'm a little teapot,
Short and stout,
Here's my handle,
Here's my spout.
When I get a steam up,
Hear me shout:
Pick me up and pour me out!

Anon.

Miss Polly Had a Dolly

Miss Polly had a dolly
   who was sick, sick, sick.
So she phoned for the doctor
   to come quick, quick, quick.
The doctor came
   with her bag and her hat,
And she knocked on the door
   with a rat-a-tat-tat.

She looked at the dolly
   and she shook her head,
And she said, 'Miss Polly,
   put her straight to bed.'
She wrote on a paper
   for a pill, pill, pill,
'I'll be back in the morning
   with my bill, bill, bill.'

Anon.

When Susie Was a Baby

When Susie was a baby, a baby Susie was.
She went, 'Goo, goo – goo, goo, goo.'

When Susie was an infant, an infant Susie was.
She went skip, skip, skippety-skip.

When Susie was a schoolgirl a schoolgirl Susie was.
She went, 'Miss, Miss, I can't do this.'

When Susie was a teenager, a teenager Susie was.
She went kiss, kiss – kiss, kiss, kiss.

When Susie was a mother, a mother Susie was.
She went rock, rock – rock, rock, rock.

When Susie was a granny, a granny Susie was.
She went, 'Knit, knit – I've lost a stitch.'

When Susie was a-dying, a-dying Susie was.
She went, 'Oooh, aah – oooh, aah, aah.'

When Susie was a skeleton, a skeleton Susie was.
She went, 'Oooooh, oooooh, ooooooh.'

When Susie was a nothing, a nothing Susie was.
She went . . .

Anon.

If You're Happy and You Know It

If you're happy and you know it,
   clap your hands.
If you're happy and you know it,
   clap your hands.
If you're happy and you know it,
   and you really want to show it,
If you're happy and you know it,
   clap your hands.
If you're happy and you know it,
   stamp your feet, *etc.*
If you're happy and you know it,
   nod your head, *etc.*
If you're happy and you know it,
   shout 'Hooray!', *etc.*

Anon.

The Wheels on the Bus

The wheels on the bus go round and round,
Round and round, round and round.
The wheels on the bus go round and round,
All day long.

The wipers on the bus go swish, swish, swish, *etc.*
The driver on the bus goes, 'Toot! Toot! Toot!', *etc.*
The conductor on the bus says: 'Hurry along please!', *etc.*
The mummies on the bus go, 'Yakkity-yak!', *etc.*
The children on the bus make TOO MUCH NOISE!, *etc.*
The babies on the bus fall fast asleep, *etc.*

Anon.

This Old Man

This old man, he played one,
He played knick-knack on my drum,
With a knick-knack paddy whack, give a dog a bone
This old man came rolling home.

This old man, he played two,
He played knick-knack on my shoe,
With a knick-knack *etc.* . . . .

This old man, he played three,
He played knick-knack on my knee,
With a knick-knack *etc.* . . . .

This old man, he played four,
He played knick-knack on my door,
With a knick-knack *etc.* . . . .

This old man, he played five,
He played knick-knack on my hide,
With a knick-knack *etc.* . . .

This old man, he played six,
He played knick-knack on some sticks,
With a knick-knack *etc.* . . .

This old man, he played seven,
He played knick-knack up in heaven,
With a knick-knack *etc.* . . .

This old man, he played eight,
He played knick-knack on my plate,
With a knick-knack *etc.* . . .

This old man, he played nine,
He played knick-knack on my spine,
With a knick-knack *etc.* . . .

This old man, he played ten,
He played knick-knack once again,
With a knick-knack *etc.* . . .

Anon.

Old Macdonald Had a Farm

Old Macdonald had a farm
E-I-E-I-O.
And on that farm he had some cows,
E-I-E-I-O.
With a moo-moo here,
And a moo-moo there,
Here a moo, there a moo,
Everywhere a moo-moo,
Old Macdonald had a farm,
E-I-E-I-O.

Old Macdonald had a farm,
E-I-E-I-O.
And on that farm he had some sheep,
E-I-E-I-O.
With a baa-baa here,
And a baa-baa there,
Here a baa, there a baa,
Everywhere a baa-baa,
Old Macdonald had a farm,
E-I-E-I-O.

Anon.

Invent more verses:
hens   – cluck-cluck
pigs   – oink-oink
dogs   – woof-woof
ducks – quack-quack
horses – neigh-neigh
etc.

Five Little Speckled Frogs

Five little speckled frogs
Sat on a speckled log
Eating the most delicious bugs –
Yum, yum.
One jumped into the pool
Where it was nice and cool,
Then there were four green speckled frogs.
Glub, glub!

Verses
Four little speckled frogs, *etc.*
Three little speckled frogs, *etc.*
Two little speckled frogs, *etc.*

One little speckled frog
Sat on a speckled log
Eating the most delicious bugs –
Yum, yum.
He jumped into the pool
Where it was nice and cool,
Now there are no green speckled frogs.
Glub, glub!

Anon.

I Have a Dog

I have a dog and his name is Rags,
He eats so much his tummy sags,
His ears flip-flop, and his tail wig-wags,
And when he walks he goes zig-zag.

Chorus
He goes flip-flop, wig-wag, zig-zag,
He goes flip-flop, wig-wag, zig-zag,
He goes flip-flop, wig-wag, zig-zag,
I love Rags and he loves me.
I love Rags and he loves me.

My dog Rags he loves to play
He rolls around in the mud all day.
I whistle but he won't obey.
He always runs the other way.

Anon.

Little Rabbit Foo Foo

Little Rabbit Foo Foo
Hopping through the green grass,
Scooping up the field mice,
And knocking them on the head.

Down came the Good Fairy
And she said:
Little Rabbit Foo Foo,
I don't want to see you
Scooping up the field mice,
And knocking them on the head;
So I'll give you four more chances.

Little Rabbit Foo Foo
I really warned you;
Now I'm going to turn you
Into a green-eyed *bug*!

Anon.

I Had a Little Monkey

I had a little monkey,
I called him Little Jim,
I put him in a bathtub,
To see if he could swim;

He drank all the water,
He ate all the soap,
He lay down on the bath mat,
Blowing bubbles from his throat.

'Mummy, mummy, I feel ill,
Call the doctor down the hill.'

In came the doctor, in came the nurse,
In came the lady with the alligator purse.

'He's naughty,' said the doctor,
'He's wicked,' said the nurse,
'Hiccups!' said the lady with the alligator purse.

Out went the doctor, out went the nurse,
Out went the lady with the alligator purse.

Anon.

Old Roger

Old Roger is dead and he lies in his grave,
Lies in his grave, lies in his grave.
Old Roger is dead and he lies in his grave,
Heigh ho, lies in his grave.

They planted an apple tree over his head,
Over his head, over his head.
They planted an apple tree over his head,
Heigh ho, over his head.

The apples grew ripe and they all tumbled down,
All tumbled down, all tumbled down.
The apples grew ripe and they all tumbled down,
Heigh ho, they all tumbled down.

There came an old woman a-picking them up,
A-picking them up, a-picking them up.
There came an old woman a-picking them up,
Heigh ho, a-picking them up.

Old Roger got up and he gave her a knock,
Gave her a knock, gave her a knock.
Old Roger got up and he gave her a knock,
Heigh ho, gave her a knock.

This made the old woman go hipperty-hop,
Hipperty-hop, hipperty-hop.
This made the old woman go hipperty-hop,
Heigh ho, hipperty-hop.

Anon.

A Frog He Would a-Wooing Go

A frog he would a-wooing go,
  Heigho, says Rowley,
Whether his mother would let him or no.
With a rowley, powley, gammon and spinach,
  Heigho, says Anthony Rowley!

So off he sets in his opera hat,
  Heigho, says Rowley,
And on the road he met with a rat.
With a rowley, powley, gammon and spinach,
  Heigho, says Anthony Rowley!

'Pray, Mr Rat, will you go with me,'
   Heigho, says Rowley,
'Kind Mrs Mousey for to see?'
With a rowley, powley, gammon and spinach,
   Heigho, says Anthony Rowley!

When they came to the door of Mousey's Hall,
   Heigho, says Rowley,
They gave a loud knock, and they gave a loud call.
With a rowley, powley, gammon and spinach,
   Heigho, says Anthony Rowley!

'Pray, Mrs Mouse, are you within?'
   Heigho, says Rowley,
'Oh yes, kind sirs, I'm sitting to spin.'
With a rowley, powley, gammon and spinach,
   Heigho, says Anthony Rowley!

'Pray, Mrs Mouse, will you give us some beer?'
   Heigho, says Rowley,
'For Froggy and I are fond of good cheer.'
With a rowley, powley, gammon and spinach,
   Heigho, says Anthony Rowley!

'Pray, Mr Frog, will you give us a song?'
   Heigho, says Rowley,
'But let it be something that's not very long.'
With a rowley, powley, gammon and spinach,
   Heigho, says Anthony Rowley!

But while they were all a-merry-making,
 Heigho, says Rowley,
A cat and her kittens came tumbling in.
With a rowley, powley, gammon and spinach,
 Heigho, says Anthony Rowley!

The cat she seized the rat by the crown;
 Heigho, says Rowley,
The kittens they pulled the little mouse down.
With a rowley, powley, gammon and spinach,
 Heigho, says Anthony Rowley!

This put Mr Frog in a terrible fright,
 Heigho, says Rowley,
He took up his hat, and wished them goodnight.
With a rowley, powley, gammon and spinach,
 Heigho, says Anthony Rowley!

But as Froggy was crossing over a brook,
 Heigho, says Rowley,
A lily-white duck came and swallowed him up.
With a rowley, powley, gammon and spinach,
 Heigho, says Anthony Rowley!

Anon.

Bobby Shaftoe

Bobby Shaftoe's gone to sea,
Silver buckles on his knee;
He'll come back and marry me,
    Bonny Bobby Shaftoe.

Bobby Shaftoe's bright and fair,
Combing down his yellow hair,
He's my ain for evermair,
    Bonny Bobby Shaftoe.

Bobby Shaftoe's tall and slim,
Always dressed so neat and trim,
The ladies they all keek at him,
    Bonny Bobby Shaftoe.

Bobby Shaftoe's getten a bairn
For to dandle in his arm;
In his arm and on his knee,
    Bonny Bobby Shaftoe.

Anon.

Soldier, Soldier, Will You Marry Me?

Oh soldier, soldier, will you marry me,
With your musket, fife, and drum?
Oh no, pretty maid, I cannot marry you,
For I have no coat to put on.

Then off she went to the tailor's shop
As fast as legs could run,
And bought him one of the very very best
And the soldier put it on.

Oh soldier, soldier, will you marry me,
With your musket, fife, and drum?
Oh no, pretty maid, I cannot marry you,
For I have no shoes to put on.

Then off she went to the cobbler's shop
As fast as legs could run,
And bought him a pair of the very very best,
And the soldier put them on.

Oh soldier, soldier, will you marry me,
With your musket, fife, and drum?
Oh no, pretty maid, I cannot marry you,
For I have no socks to put on.

Then off she went to the sock-maker's shop
As fast as legs could run,
And bought him a pair of the very very best,
And the soldier put them on.

Oh soldier, soldier, will you marry me,
With your musket, fife, and drum?
Oh no, pretty maid, I cannot marry you,
For I have no hat to put on.

Then off she went to the hatter's shop
As fast as legs could run,
And bought him one of the very very best,
And the soldier put it on.

Oh soldier, soldier, will you marry me,
With your musket, fife, and drum?
Oh no, pretty maid, I cannot marry you,
For I have a wife at home.

Anon.

Old Noah's Ark

Old Noah once he built an ark,
And patched it up with hickory bark.
He anchored it to a great big rock,
And then he began to load up his stock.

The animals went in one by one,
The elephant chewing a carroway bun.

The animals went in two by two,
The crocodile and the kangaroo.

The animals went in three by three,
The tall giraffe and the tiny flea.

The animals went in four by four,
The hippopotamus stuck in the door.

The animals went in five by five,
The bees mistook the bear for a hive.

The animals went in six by six,
The monkey was up to his usual tricks.

The animals went in seven by seven,
Said the ant to the elephant, 'Who're ye shoving?'

The animals went in eight by eight,
Some were early and some were late.

The animals went in nine by nine,
They all formed fours and marched in line.

The animals went in ten by ten,
If you want any more, you can read it again.

Anon.

There Was an Old Lady

There was an old lady who swallowed a fly.
I don't know why she swallowed a fly.
Perhaps she'll die.

The same old lady, she swallowed a spider
That wriggled and jiggled and tickled inside her.
She swallowed the spider to catch the fly.
I don't know why she swallowed a fly.
Perhaps she'll die.

The same old lady, she swallowed a bird.
How absurd to swallow a bird!
She swallowed the bird to catch the spider,
She swallowed the spider to catch the fly.
I don't know why she swallowed a fly.
Perhaps she'll die.

The same old lady, she swallowed a cat.
Fancy that! She swallowed a cat.
She swallowed the cat to catch the bird.
She swallowed the bird to catch the spider,
She swallowed the spider to catch the fly.
I don't know why she swallowed a fly.
Perhaps she'll die.

The same old lady, she swallowed a dog.
She went the whole hog when she swallowed the dog.
She swallowed the dog to catch the cat,
She swallowed the cat to catch the bird,
She swallowed the bird to catch the spider,
She swallowed the spider to catch the fly.
I don't know why she swallowed a fly.
Perhaps she'll die.

The same old lady, she swallowed a cow.
I don't know how she swallowed the cow.
She swallowed the cow to catch the dog,
She swallowed the dog to catch the cat,
She swallowed the cat to catch the bird,
She swallowed the bird to catch the spider,
She swallowed the spider to catch the fly.
I don't know why she swallowed a fly.
Perhaps she'll die.

The same old lady, she swallowed a horse.
She died, of course.

Anon.

The Mouse, the Frog and
the Little Red Hen

Once a Mouse, a Frog and a Little Red Hen,
Together kept a house;
The Frog was the laziest of frogs,
And lazier still was the Mouse.

The work all fell on the Little Red Hen,
Who had to get the wood,
And build the fires, and scrub, and cook,
And sometimes hunt the food.

One day, as she went scratching round,
She found a bag of rye;
Said she, 'Now who will make some bread?'
Said the lazy Mouse, 'Not I.'

'Nor I,' croaked the Frog as he drowsed in the shade,
Red Hen made no reply,
But flew around with bowl and spoon,
And mixed and stirred the rye.

'Who'll make the fire to bake the bread?'
Said the Mouse again, 'Not I,'
And, scarcely opening his sleepy eyes,
Frog made the same reply.

The Little Red Hen said never a word,
But a roaring fire she made;
And while the bread was baking brown,
'Who'll set the table?' she said.

'Not I,' said the sleepy Frog with a yawn;
'Nor I,' said the Mouse again.
So the table she set and the bread put on,
'Who'll eat this bread?' said the Hen.

'I will!' cried the Frog. 'And I!' squeaked the Mouse,
As they near the table drew:
'Oh, no, you won't!' said the Little Red Hen,
And away with the loaf she flew.

Anon.

Nobody Loves Me

Nobody loves me,
Everybody hates me,
Think I'll go and eat worms.

Big fat squishy ones,
Little thin skinny ones,
See how they wriggle and squirm.

Bite their heads off.
'Schlurp!' They're lovely,
Throw their tails away.

Nobody knows
How big I grows
On worms three times a day.

Anon.

On Top of Spaghetti

On top of spaghetti, all covered with cheese,
I lost my poor meatball when somebody sneezed.

It rolled off the table, and on to the floor,
And then my poor meatball rolled out of the door.

It rolled in the garden, and under a bush,
And then my poor meatball was nothing but mush.

The mush was as tasty, as tasty can be,
And early next summer, it grew into a tree.

The tree was all covered with beautiful moss,
It grew lovely meatballs and tomato sauce.

So if you eat spaghetti, all covered with cheese,
Hold on to your meatball, and don't ever sneeze.

Anon.

Dipping, Skipping and Clapping

Eeny Meeny Miny Moe

Eeny meeny miny moe
Catch a tiger by the toe.
If he hollers let him go.
Eeny meeny miny moe.

Anon.

One Potato

One potato
Two potato
Three potato
Four –
Five potato
Six potato
Seven potato
More.

Anon.

Abna Babna

Abna Babna
Lady-Snee
Ocean potion
Sugar and tea
Potato roast
And English toast
Out goes she.

Anon.

Icker Backer

Icker backer,
Soda cracker,
Icker backer boo,
Engine number nine,
Out goes you.

Anon.

Ipper Dipper Dation

Ipper dipper dation,
My operation.
How many people at the station?

The one who comes to number . . . five
Will surely not be IT.
One, two, three, four, five.

Anon.

Inky Pinky Ponky

Inky pinky ponky
Daddy bought a donkey.
The donkey died,
Daddy cried,
Inky pinky ponky.

Anon.

Ip, Dip

Ip, dip, sky blue
Who's It? Not you.
Not because you're dirty
Not because you're clean
Not because your mother says
You're the fairy queen
So O-U-T you must go.

Anon.

Did You Ever Tell a Lie?

Did you ever tell a lie?
No.
Yes, you did, you know you did,
You stole my mother's teapot lid.
What colour was it?
(Insert colour)
No it wasn't, it was gold
That's another lie you've told
So out you must go.

Anon.

Ibble Wobble

Ibble wobble black bobble,
Ibble wobble out,
Turn the dirty dishcloth
Inside out –
First you turn it inside,
Then you turn it out –
Ibble wobble black bobble,
Ibble wobble out.

Anon.

I Like Silver

I like silver
I like brass
I like looking
In the looking-glass.

I like rubies
I like pearls
I like wearing
My hair in curls.

Anon.

Bumper Car

Bumper car, bumper car
Number 48,
Whizzed round the cooooorner . . .

. . . And slammed on the brakes.

Brakes didn't work,
Slid down the hill,
Landed in the duck pond
And then stood still.
How many fishes can you see?
One, two, three, four, five . . .

Anon.

Blue Bells, Cockle Shells

Blue bells, cockle shells,
Eavy, Ivy, O-ver,
The boys are in the clover.
Mother's in the kitchen,
Doing all the stitchin'.
How many stitches can she do?
One, two, three, four, five . . .

Anon.

Early in the Morning

Early in the morning at half past eight,
I heard the mailman knocking at the gate,
Up jumps *Poppy* to open up the door
How many letters fell on the floor?
One, two, three, four, five . . .

Who from?
A, B, C, D, E . . .

Anon.

I'm a Girl Scout

I'm a little girl scout, dressed in blue,
Here are the actions I must do.
Salute to the captain,
Bow to the Queen,
Turn right round
And count sixteen.
One, two, three . . . sixteen.

Anon.

Underneath the Apple Tree

Underneath the apple tree
A boy said to me –
Kiss me, cuddle me,
Who should it be?
A, B, C, D . . .
Will you get married?
Yes, No, Yes, No . . .
What will he marry you in?
Silk, satin, cotton, rags . . .
How will you go to your wedding?
Coach, carriage, wheelbarrow, car . . .
How many children?
One, two, three, four, five . . .

Anon.

73

Teddy Bear

Teddy bear, teddy bear,
  Turn around.
Teddy bear, teddy bear,
  Touch the ground.

Teddy bear, teddy bear,
  Hands on head.
Teddy bear, teddy bear,
  Go to bed.

Teddy bear, teddy bear,
  Jump the stairs.
Teddy bear, teddy bear,
  Say your prayers.

Teddy bear, teddy bear,
  Turn out the light.
Teddy bear, teddy bear,
  Spell goodnight.

G-O-O-D-N-I-G-H-T

Anon.

I Went to the Animal Fair

I went to the animal fair,
The birds and the beasts were there.
By the light of the moon the gay baboon
Was combing his golden hair.
The monkey fell out of his bunk
And slid down the elephant's trunk.
The elephant sneezed
And fell on his knees
But what became of the monkey,
Monkey, monkey,
Monkey, monkey,
Monkey, monk!

Anon.

Not Last Night

Not last night
But the night before
Twenty-four robbers
Came knocking at my door.
Went downstairs to let them in
And this is what I saw:

Spanish lady, Spanish lady
Do high kicks.

Spanish lady, Spanish lady,
Take a bow.

Spanish lady, Spanish lady,
That's all for now.

Anon.

Have You Ever

Have you ever ever ever
In your long-legged life
Seen a long-legged sailor
With a long-legged wife?

No, I've never never never
In my long-legged life
Seen a long-legged sailor
With a long-legged wife.

Anon.

A Sailor Went to Sea Sea Sea

A sailor went to sea sea sea
To see what he could see see see
But all that he could see see see
Was the bottom of the deep blue sea sea sea.

A sailor went to chop chop chop
To see what he could chop chop chop
But all that he could chop chop chop
Was the bottom of the deep blue chop chop chop.

A sailor went to knee knee knee
To see what he could knee knee knee
But all that he could knee knee knee
Was the bottom of the deep blue knee knee knee.

A sailor went to sea, chop, knee
To see what he could sea, chop, knee
But all that he could sea, chop, knee
Was the bottom of the deep blue sea, chop, knee.

Anon.

Three, Six, Nine

Three, six, nine,
The goose drank wine,
The monkey chewed tobacco
On the street car line.
The line broke,
The monkey got choked,
And they all went to heaven
In a little row boat.

Anon.

I'm Popeye the Sailor Man

I'm Popeye the sailor man, *full stop,*
I live in a caravan, *full stop.*
I opened the door and fell flat on the floor,
I'm Popeye the sailor man, *full stop,*
Comma comma, dash dash, full stop.

Anon.

Dom Dom Malayas

Dom dom malayas,
Sweet sweet malayas,
Sweet sweet lady,
Gimme, gimme chocomilk,
Chocomilk is out.
One, two, three.

Anon.

I Went to a Chinese Restaurant

I went to a Chinese restaurant
To buy a loaf of bread bread bread.
They wrapped it up in a five-pound note
And this is what they said said said:

My . . . name . . . is . . .
Eli Eli,
Chickeni Chickeni,
I can do the cancan just like this,
I can do the hula hoop, I can do the twist;
Queens go curtsey,
Kings go bow,
Boys go kiss kiss,
Girls go WOW!

Anon.

Jamaican Clap Rhyme

Where your mamma gone?
She gone down town.

She take any money?
She take ten pound.

When your mamma come back,
what she gonna bring back?

Hats and frocks and
shoes and socks.

Anon.

Let's Get the Rhythm of the Street

Let's get the rhythm of the street –
Doctor Knickerbocker, Knickerbocker,
 Number ten!

Mime actions for each verse.

Now we've got the rhythm of the street,
Let's get the rhythm of the feet –
 STAMP STAMP!

Now we've got the rhythm of the feet –
 STAMP STAMP!
Let's get the rhythm of the hands –
 CLAP CLAP!

Now we've got the rhythm of the hands –
 CLAP CLAP!
Let's get the rhythm of the hips –
 WHOOOWEEE!

Now we've got the rhythm of the hips –
 WHOOOWEEE!
Let's get the rhythm of the nose –
 BEEP BEEP!

Now we've got the rhythm of the nose –
 BEEP BEEP!

Put it all together and see what we've got –
STAMP STAMP, CLAP CLAP,
   WHOOOWEEE, BEEP BEEP!

Let's get the rhythm of the street –
Doctor Knickerbocker, Knickerbocker,
   Number ten!

Anon.

Other actions:

knees	– slap knees
cheeks	– puff cheeks out
tongue	– stick tongue out
teeth	– bite teeth
eyes	– blink
head	– nod
hot dog	– pant droopily
tired teacher	– snore snore!

Counting Rhymes

One, Two, Three

One, two, three,
Father caught a flea.
Put it in a teapot
To make a cup of tea.

The flea jumped out,
Mother gave a shout,
In came Billy
With his shirt hanging out.

Anon.

Five Old Fishermen

Five old fishermen
Sitting on a bridge
One caught a tiddler
One caught a fridge.

One caught a tadpole
One caught an eel
And the fifth one caught
A perambulator wheel.

Anon.

85

Ten in the Bed

There were ten in the bed
And the little one said,
'Roll over, roll over.'
So they all rolled over
And one fell out . . .

There were nine in the bed
(keep going . . . until final verse)

There was one in the bed
And the little one said,
'I've done it! I've done it!'

Anon.

Five Currant Buns

Five currant buns in a baker's shop,
Round and fat with sugar on top.
Along came . . . *(name a child)* with a penny one day,
Bought a currant bun and took it away.

Four currant buns in a baker's shop,
Round and fat with sugar on top.
Along came . . . *(name another child)* with a penny one day,
Bought a currant bun and took it away.

(keep going till last verse)

No currant buns in a baker's shop,
Big and fat with sugar on the top.
Along came . . . *(name one more child)* with a penny one
   day,
No currant buns, so *she/he* went right away.

Anon.

Ten Fat Sausages

Ten fat sausages sizzling in the pan,
Ten fat sausages sizzling in the pan.
One went POP! and the other went BANG!
Then there were eight fat sausages sizzling in the pan.

Eight fat sausages sizzling in the pan,
Eight fat sausages sizzling in the pan.
One went POP! and the other went BANG!
Then there were six fat sausages sizzling in the pan.
(keep going till none are left)

Anon.

One, Two, Three, Four, Five

One, two, three, four, five,
Once I caught a fish alive.

Six, seven, eight, nine, ten,
Then I let him go again.

Why did you let him go?
Because he bit my finger so!

Which finger did he bite?
This little finger on the right!

Anon.

Ten Green Bottles

Ten green bottles hanging on the wall,
Ten green bottles hanging on the wall,
And if one green bottle should accidentally fall,
There'd be nine green bottles hanging on the wall.

Nine green bottles hanging on the wall,
Nine green bottles hanging on the wall,
And if one green bottle should accidentally fall,
There'd be eight green bottles hanging on the wall.
(keep going till one is left)

One green bottle hanging on the wall,
One green bottle hanging on the wall,
And if one green bottle should accidentally fall,
There'd be *no* green bottles hanging on the wall.

Anon.

One, Two, Buckle My Shoe

One, two,
Buckle my shoe;
Three, four,
Knock at the door;
Five, six,
Pick up sticks;
Seven, eight,
Lay them straight;
Nine, ten,
A big fat hen;
Eleven, twelve,
Dig and delve;
Thirteen, fourteen,
Maids a-courting;
Fifteen, sixteen,
Maids in the kitchen;
Seventeen, eighteen,
Maids in waiting;
Nineteen, twenty,
My plate's empty.

Anon.

Monday's Child

Monday's child is fair of face,
Tuesday's child is full of grace,
Wednesday's child is full of woe,
Thursday's child has far to go,
Friday's child is loving and giving,
Saturday's child works hard for a living,
But the child that is born on the Sabbath day
is bonny and blithe and good and gay.

Anon.

Solomon Grundy

Solomon Grundy
Born on a Monday,
Christened on Tuesday,
Married on Wednesday,
Took ill on Thursday,
Worse on Friday,
Died on Saturday,
Buried on Sunday.
That was the end
Of Solomon Grundy.

Anon.

Thirty Days Hath September

Thirty days hath September,
April, June, and November.
All the rest have thirty-one,
Except February alone,
Which has four and twenty-four
Till leap-year gives it one day more.

Anon.

Tongue-twisters

Six Tongue-twisters

Red leather, yellow leather.

The Leith police dismisseth us.

Three grey geese in a green field grazing.

Around the rugged rocks, the ragged rascal ran.

Sister Susie's sewing shirts for sailors.

How much wood would a woodchuck chuck
If a woodchuck could chuck wood?

Anon.

She Sells Seashells

She sells seashells by the seashore.
The shells that she sells are seashells, I'm sure.
So if she sells seashells by the seashore,
I'm sure that the shells are seashore shells.

Anon.

I Saw Esau

I saw Esau sawing wood,
And Esau saw I saw him;
Though Esau saw I saw him saw,
Still Esau went on sawing.

Anon.

Peter Piper

Peter Piper picked a peck of pickled pepper;
Did Peter Piper pick a peck of pickled pepper?
If Peter Piper picked a peck of pickled pepper,
Where's the peck of pickled pepper Peter Piper picked?

Anon.

The Swan

Swan swam over the sea –
Swim, swan, swim;
Swan swam back again,
Well swum, swan.

Anon.

Peter, Peter, Pumpkin Eater

Peter, Peter, pumpkin eater,
Had a wife and couldn't keep her;
Put her in a pumpkin shell,
And there he kept her very well.

Anon.

Betty Botter

Betty Botter bought some butter,
But, she said, this butter's bitter;
If I put it in my batter,
It will make my batter bitter,
But a bit of better butter
Will make my batter better.
So she bought a bit of butter
Better than her bitter butter,
And she put it in her batter,
And it made her batter better,
So 'twas better Betty Botter
Bought a bit of better butter.

Anon.

Bizzy Buzzy Bee

Bizzy buzzy bumble bee
Busy buzzing busily.

Busybody bumble bee
Busy buzzing noisily.

Bustling buzzy bumble bee
Busy busy as can be.

Bizzy buzzy bumble bee
Busy buzzing busily.

John Foster

Sue Shore

Sue Shore shrieked.
Sue Shore shouted, 'Shoo!'
Sue was sure she saw
A shrew in her shoe.

John Foster

Shaun Short

Shaun Short bought some shorts.
The shorts were shorter than Shaun Short thought.
Shaun Short's short shorts were so short
Shaun Short thought, 'Shaun, you ought
Not to have bought shorts so short.'

John Foster

Dick's Dog

Dick had a dog
The dog dug
The dog dug deep
How deep did Dick's dog dig?

Dick had a duck
The duck dived
The duck dived deep
How deep did Dick's duck dive?

Dick's duck dived as deep as Dick's dog dug.

Trevor Millum

Riddle Me Ree

Humpty-Dumpty

Humpty-Dumpty sat on a wall
Humpty-Dumpty had a great fall
All the King's horses and all the King's men
Couldn't put Humpty together again.

Anon.

As I Went over Lincoln Bridge

As I went over Lincoln Bridge,
I met Mister Rusticap,
Pins and needles on his back,
A-going to Thorney fair.

Anon.

Four Riddles

Riddle me, riddle me,
What is that:
Over the head
And under the hat?

Thirty white horses
Upon a white hill,
Now they dance,
Now they prance,
Now they stand still.

Tall and thin,
Red within,
Nail on top
And there it is.

A house full,
A hole full,
You cannot gather
A bowl full.

Anon.

Adventures with Pirates, Ghosts and Aliens

The Cave

Can you be daring?
Can you be brave?
Will you come down
to explore the cave?

We'll put on our boots
and carefully tramp
down through the darkness,
all slimy and damp.

They say there's a chest
a hundred years old.
It's spilling over
with jewels and gold.

The pirates left it
and never returned.
Their ship caught fire
and the map got burned.

So I'll take the torch
and you take the sack.
Let's go down there
and bring some back.

But hush! There's a dragon
who just might waken,
if he hears any of it
being taken.

Tony Mitton

I Wish I Was a Pirate

I wish I was a pirate
  With a long beard hanging down,
A cutlass dangling from my belt,
  My teeth all black and brown.

A parrot on my shoulder,
  A patch upon one eye,
A pirate ship to sail on,
  A pirate flag to fly.

The rolling waves would be my home,
  I'd live through many wrecks.
I'd always have the best of maps –
  The ones marked with an X!

Pirates don't have parents,
  They don't get sent to school.
They never have to take a bath,
  For them there are no rules.

Yo-ho-ho me hearties!
   It's a pirate's life for me . . .
Pistols in my pockets,
   Salt-pork for my tea!

Tony Bradman

Sitting in My Bath-tub

Sitting in my bath-tub,
I have sailed the seven seas.
I have anchored by the taps.
I've been shipwrecked off the knees.

I have sailed into the unknown
To beat off an attack
From a fleet of pirates
Round behind my back.

I have sailed between the fingers
Where no other ship has been.
I've explored the murky depths
In a soapy submarine.

Sitting in my bath-tub
I have sailed the seven seas.
I have anchored by the taps.
I've been shipwrecked off the knees.

John Foster

Alone in the Grange

Strange,
Strange,
Is the little old man
Who lives in the Grange.
Old,
Old;
And they say that he keeps
A box full of gold.
Bowed,
Bowed,
Is his thin little back
That once was so proud.

Soft,
Soft,
Are his steps as he climbs
The stairs to the loft.
Black,
Black,
Is the old shuttered house.
Does he sleep on a sack?

They say he does magic,
That he can cast spells,
That he prowls round the garden
Listening for bells;
That he watches for strangers,
Hates every soul,
And peers with his dark eye
Through the keyhole.

I wonder, I wonder,
As I lie in my bed,
Whether he sleeps with his hat on his head?
Is he really magician
With altar of stone,
Or a lonely old gentleman
Left on his own?

Gregory Harrison

Who's Afraid?

Do I have to go haunting tonight?
The children might give me a fright.
It's dark in that house.
I might meet a mouse.
Do I have to go haunting tonight?

I don't like the way they scream out,
When they see me skulking about.
I'd rather stay here,
Where there's nothing to fear.
Do I have to go haunting tonight?

John Foster

Spooky House

Listen, hear the creak
    of the old floorboard.
Look, see the gleam
    of the sharp-edged sword.
Sniff, smell the dust
    in the stale, damp air.
Touch, feel the cobwebs
    hanging down the dark stair.

Do I hear a ghost
    tapping on the windowpane?
No, it's just my brother's
    teeth chattering again!

Penny Kent

Who's Counting?

One for a shadow
Two for a scare
Three for a cobweb
    in my hair.

Four for a whisper
Five for a scream
Six for a monster
    in my dream.

Seven for a shiver
up my spine:
Reach for the light switch –
just in time!

Celia Warren

Going Upstairs

Only the bravest person dares
To go up the trickety, rickety stairs.

The first step creaks like a bending bone.
On the second there's a stain.
You have to miss the third step out
Or you'll never come down again.

Only the bravest person dares
To go up the trickety, rickety stairs.

Hold your breath on the fourth step.
On the fifth step count to five.
Close your eyes on the sixth step
Or you'll never come down alive.

Only the bravest person dares
To go up the trickety, rickety stairs.

Left foot on the seventh,
On the eighth your right.
Once you reach the ninth step
Your bedroom door's in sight.

Safely on the landing
Keep a steady head:
Cross your fingers as you go
And jump into bed.

Phew!

Celia Warren

The Ghost in the Castle

The ghost in the castle
　　tu-whit tu-whoo
walks down the stairs.
　　He's looking at you.

The ghost in the castle
　　clank clank rattle
is a knight who was killed
　　long ago in battle.

The ghost in the castle
　　tap tap creak
makes your hair stand on end
　　and your legs go weak.

114

But you can walk through him
   (you can if you dare)
for the ghost in the castle
   is not really there.

          Charles Thomson

Wizard

Under my bed I keep a box
With seven locks,

And all the things I have to hide
Are safe inside:

My rings, my wand, my hat, my spells,
My book of spells.

I could fit a mountain into a shoe
If I wanted to,

Or put the sea in a paper cup
And drink it up.

I could change a cushion into a bird
With a magic word,

Or turn December into spring,
Or make stones sing,

I could clap my hands and watch the moon,
Like a white balloon,

Come floating to my window-sill . . .
One day I will.

Richard Edwards

Monster

I saw a monster in the woods
As I was cycling by,
His footsteps smouldered in the leaves,
His breath made bushes die,

And when he raised his hairy arm
It blotted out the sun;
He snatched a pigeon from the sky
And swallowed it in one.

His mouth was like a dripping cave,
His eyes like pools of lead,
And when he growled I rode back home
And rushed upstairs to bed.

But that was yesterday and though
It gave me quite a fright,
I'm older now and braver so
I'm going back tonight.

116

I'll tie him up when he's asleep
And take him to the zoo.
The trouble is he's rather big . . .
Will you come too?

Richard Edwards

The Mystery Space Beasts

They live on a planet
not far from the Sun.
Some fly through the air
while others just run.

Some have big heads
which are hairless as tin
while others have hair
which sprouts from their skin.

They dig food from dirt,
and gobble dead meat;
the young squeal like pigs
if you tickle their feet.

They slurp, burp, and grunt;
their manners are bad.
Their eyes become waterfalls
when they feel sad.

117

They come in most colours,
some yellow, some white.
Some dye their hair pink
and do look a sight.

These creatures vary
from tiny to tall,
and in salty water
they've been known to crawl.

Well, who are these space beasts?
Can't you guess who?
The answer is easy:
it's you, you, and YOU!

Wes Magee

Spaceship Shop

I need to find a spaceship shop
I want to buy a rocket
One that's sleek and shiny
With a key so I can lock it

My aim is to travel
As high as I can go
Then land on a peaceful planet
Leap out and say 'Hello!'

I won't stay in space too long
With bright stars all around me
I know if I'm not home on time
Mum is bound to ground me

But first, I need to find that spaceship shop
So I can buy a rocket
One that's sleek and shiny
With a key so I can lock it

Note: Make sure that its brakes work
        I'll crash if I can't stop it!

Bernard Young

Rocket Boy

At night
I am captain
of an alien crew,
on my red and silver rocket
speeding

through stars.
Behind closed eyes
I, the bold explorer,
fly past pulsing purple planets,
spinning

119

with rings
emerald moons.
I dodge space dust, comets,
bronze and gold starbursts, exploding
white dwarfs.

At night
I am captain
of an alien crew
'til I'm sucked inside the black hole
of sleep.

Celia Gentles

The Really Rocking Rocket Trip

We're off in a rocket
A silver, shiny rocket
Zooming in our rocket
Just you and me
Racing in our rocket
Our really rocking rocket
Rolling in our rocket
What a lot we'll see!

Land on Jupiter, play with some aliens
Land on Neptune, swim in the sea
Land on Venus, play kissy-kissy chase
Land on Mars, chocolate bars in every tree
Land on Mercury, take the temperature
Land on Saturn, 'cos it's Saturday
Land on Uranus, play tiggy in our space suits
Land on Pluto, hip-hip-hooray!

Back to our rocket
Our wonderful rocket
Away in our rocket
Just you and me
Blast off in our rocket
Our supersonic rocket
Land in the garden
Just in time for tea!

David Harmer

The Alien's Sweet Shop

He sells Asteroid Crunch
And Galaxy Munch
And Flying Saucer Dips.

He has Chocolate Zooms
And Peppermint Moons
And Spaceship Lollies to lick.

There are Pluto Creams
And Jupiter Dreams
And Twinkling Stardust Bars.

But his Milky Way Treats
That are heaven to eat
Are my favourite sweets by far.

Cynthia Rider

My Spaceship

I've a picture of Pluto,
My white spacesuit,
My robot Charlie,
My red moon-boots,
All hidden tight,
In my secret lair,
My spaceship under the stairs.

Not even Mum,
Nor my sister Sal,
Not even Dad,
Nor my brother Cal,
Can come with me,
To my secret lair,
My spaceship under the stairs.

122

I can jet to the moon,
  Or fly to Mars,
    Take my shuttle,
      Or my solar car,
        Shout, 'We have lift-off!'
         On a faraway star,
In my spaceship under the stairs.

I can catch a comet,
  Or a meteorite,
    Zoom round and round,
      A satellite,
        Do what I want,
         Whenever I like,
In my spaceship under the stairs.

It's my special place,
  When I creep inside,
    To play or think
      To dream or hide,
        Or just to be there,
         With my old cloth bear,
In my spaceship under the stairs.

Mary Green

The Alien

On my way to school I saw an alien.
No you didn't, said Billy.

I saw an alien with two heads.
No you didn't, said Jake.

I saw an alien with two heads and four arms.
No you didn't, said Ed.

I saw an alien with two heads, four arms and six eyes.
No you didn't, said Harriet.

I saw an alien with two heads, four arms, six eyes and eight
    legs.
No you didn't, said Ali.

OH YES HE DID,
Said the alien.

And everyone said,

aaaaaaaaaAAAAAAAAAAAAHHHHHHHHHHH!!

Roger Stevens

Holiday Trip . . . in the 21st Century

You'll take a break on Venus,
it's lava-hot in June,
then join an all-night party
on the dark side of the Moon.

You'll sail through storms on Saturn,
and trudge the sands of Mars,
then zoom away to Neptune
and tour some distant stars.

You'll skate on icy Pluto
and ski for all you're worth,
then when the hols are over
you'll
     fly
        right
           back
               to
                  Earth.

Wes Magee

Mrs Sprockett's Strange Machine

Mrs Sprockett has a strange machine.
It will thrill you through and through.
It's got wheels and springs and seven strings
And this is what they do.

Pull string number one . . .
. . . it begins to hum   mmmm mmmmmmmm
Pull string number two . . .
. . . it goes **COCK A DOODLE DOO.**
Pull string number three . . .
. . . it will buzz like a bee   zzzzzzzzzzzz
Pull string number four . . .
. . . it will start to **ROAR.**
Pull string number five . . .
. . . it will dip and dive.
Pull string number six . . .
. . . it will play silly tricks.
Pull string number seven . . .
. . . it will fly up to heaven.

Mrs Sprockett has a strange machine.
It will thrill you through and through.
It's got wheels and springs and seven strings
And . . . **I WISH I HAD ONE TOO!**

Michaela Morgan

Rickety Train Ride

I'm taking the train to Ricketywick.
Clickety clickety clack.
I'm sat in my seat
with a sandwich to eat
as I travel the trickety track.

It's an ever so rickety trickety train,
and I honestly thickety think
that before it arrives
at the end of the line
it will tip up my drippety drink.

Tony Mitton

The Engine Driver

The train goes running along the line,
    Jicketty-can, jicketty-can.
I wish it were mine, I wish it were mine,
    Jicketty-can, jicketty-can.
The engine driver stands in front –
    He makes it run, he makes it shunt.

127

Out of the town,
Out of the town,
Over the hill,
Over the down,
Under the bridges,
Across the lea,
Over the ridges
And down to the sea.

With a jicketty-can, jicketty-can,
Jicketty-jicketty-jicketty-can,
Jicketty-can, jicketty-can . . .

Clive Sansom

Fairies, Princesses
and Mermaids

A Bedtime Rhyme for Young Fairies
(Whispered to Clare in a dream)

One tired fairy,
Two folded wings,
Three magic wishes,
Four daisy rings,
Five moonlight dancers,
Six starlight spells,
Seven hidden treasures,
Eight silver bells,
Nine secret doorways,
Ten keys to keep,
And one little fairy
Fast asleep.

Clare Bevan

The Song of the Naughty Fairies
(Clare found this poem when she was looking for a lost sock.)

Some fairies are charming and gentle and sweet
Some fairies go dancing on little, light feet.

But we are the fairies
Who tangle your hair,
Who jumble your jigsaws
When no one is there,
Who hide your best treasures,
Who muddle your socks,
Who tumble your toys
From their big, tidy box,
Who tickle your hamster,
Who startle your cat,
Who drop spiky stones
On your soft, bedside mat,
Who scamper and giggle
Like rascally mice,
Who aren't very dainty.
Who aren't very nice.

Some fairies just twinkle and skip in the sun,
But WE are the Fairies who have the most FUN.

Clare Bevan

Fairy Names

(When Clare found this poem, all the names had been crossed out . . . except for one!)

What shall we call the Fairy Child?

Mouse-Fur? Cat's Purr?
Weasel-Wild?

Bat-Wing? Bee-Sting?
Shining River?
Snakebite? Starlight?
Stone? Or Shiver?

Acorn? Frogspawn?
Golden Tree?
Snowflake? Daybreak?
Stormy Sea?

Snail-Shell? Harebell?
Scarlet Flame?

How shall we choose the Fairy's name?

Clare Bevan

A Fairy Alphabet

(Young fairies learn this poem before
they write their first letters.)

Aiming high and swooping low,
Building castles in the snow,
Casting spells with shiny thorns,
Drifting over garden lawns,
Eating berries dipped in honey,
Finding teeth and leaving money,
Gliding on a summer breeze,
Hiding inside hollow trees,
Icing tiny fairy cakes,
Jumping over moonlit lakes,
Keeping still when danger's near,
Leaping with the fallow deer,
Making children's dreams come true,
Nursing injured mouse and shrew,
Opening a toadstool door,
Pirouetting round the floor,
Quivering the cobweb strands,
Riding moths to magic lands,
Singing charms in stormy weather,
Twisting ivy threads together,
Using leaves for autumn games,
Vanishing like candle flames,
Wearing shoes with feathered wings,

Xercising bugs on strings,
Yachting down the woodland streams

AND

Zig-zag-dancing in your dreams.

Clare Bevan

Fairy Letters
(These letters were once sent to Clare and her lazy old cat.)

Dear Giants
(In your Giant House)
Have you seen
My racing mouse?
His eyes are sharp,
His fur is black,
If you find him –
Send him back.

Dear Giants
(And your Giant Cat)
My mouse came home!
He's grown quite fat
And rather slow
But never mind –
Thank you all
For being kind.

Dear Giants
Here is your REWARD!
A magic cake
(It's slightly gnawed).
Now – take one bite
And make three wishes.
P.S. My mouse
Sends love and kisses.

Clare Bevan

What Do the Fairies Ride?
(Clare would really like to ride on a heron.)

The quietest fairies ride barn owls
As soft as a flurry of snow,
The fiercest fairies ride falcons,
Or sometimes a cackling crow.

The cleverest fairies ride magpies,
The tiniest fairies ride wrens,
The happiest fairies ride songbirds,
The noisiest fairies ride hens.

The sleepiest fairies ride dormice,
The funniest fairies ride frogs,
The bravest of fairies ride whirlwinds,
Or cling to the collars of dogs.

The fairies who grant all our wishes,
They ride on the greyest of doves,
The fairies who ride on the Phoenix
Wear feathery, fireproof gloves.

The Fairies of Morning ride skylarks.
The Fairies of Darkness ride bats,
The Fairies of Water ride fishes,
The Fairies of Moonlight ride cats.

But the daintiest rider who soars through the sky
Is the Fairy of May on her blue butterfly.

Clare Bevan

Ten Fairy Facts
*(These facts were given to Clare
by a Bumble Bee called Hum.)*

1. The best spider to use for Tree-Falling is the Wolf Spider.
   (She's much friendlier than she sounds.)
2. Fairies like to wear Conker-Shell Helmets for games
   lessons. (The straps are made from sticky cobwebs.)
3. The Pond Fairy has two new babies. The girl is called
   Lake-Lily and the boy is called Frog-Rider.
4. The biggest tooth the fairies have collected this year
   came from a young polar bear called Growler.
5. Flittery-Flutter-Forget-Me-Not-Blue says the secret of
   long life is one new Fairy Joke every day.

6. The Fairy Queen's favourite book is 'One Hundred Amazing Eyelash Spells'.
7. The Snow Fairy hurt her wings in a Christmas blizzard, but she was given a really good spell and now she can fly faster than ever.
8. Fairies NEVER wear leafy hats when they dance with a hamster.
9. The Fairy of Bees says that stripy, velvet slippers will be very popular this winter.
10. If you hear jingly music at the end of your garden this summer, please don't worry. It's only the Fairy Fairground.

Clare Bevan

A Flutter of Fairies
(Collected by Clare)

A flutter of fairies.
A whisper of wings.
A shiver of cobwebs.
A spangle of rings.
A canter of horse flies.
A rumble of bees.
A splatter of frogs.
A city of trees.
A village of toadstools.
An ocean of ponds.

A procession of snails.
A sparkle of wands.
A glimmer of glow-worms.
A treasure of dew.
A shower of wishes
For me. And for you.

Clare Bevan

A School Report
(From the Hollow Tree Charm School for Fairy Children.
Hidden inside Clare's hollow tree)

Name: F. Thunderfoot

Subject – Dancing:

Fairy Thunderfoot always does her best.
She has tried VERY hard
To balance on a moonbeam,
To spin on the top of a pin,
To skip in neat circles,
But, sadly, she failed her Dancing Test
When she toppled off her toadstool.

Subject – Cooking:

Fairy Thunderfoot always does her best.
She has tried VERY hard
Not to lick her silver spoon,
Not to spill her fairy dust,
Not to stir her wand QUITE so fast,
But, sadly, she failed her Fairy Cake Test
When she accidentally ate them all.

Subject – Tooth-Finding:

Fairy Thunderfoot always does her best.
She has tried VERY hard
To tiptoe round rooms without giggling,
To peep under pillows without sneezing,
To count shiny coins without dropping them,
But, sadly, she failed her Tooth Fairy Test
When she sat on a squeaky teddy bear.

Subject – Spelling And Sparkling:

Fairy Thunderfoot always does her best.
She has tried VERY hard
To grant wishes for worried children,
To weave dreams for sleepy children,
To cast cheerful spells for sad children,
And, happily, she has passed her Fairy Godmother Test
With a shower of golden stars.

Clare Bevan

The Mouse-rider's Rap
(This mouse-race was secretly watched by Clare.)

Harness your mouse,
And cling to his fur,
Wait for the sound
Of the tomcat's purr,
Then gallop away
Under the trees,
Leap over the molehills
Faster than fleas,
Swerve down the track
Where a cat can't follow,
Twist and turn to
The hidden hollow,
Skid and scramble
Around the lawn,
Jump the nettles
And dodge the yawn
Of the sleeping dog
With his yellow fangs,
Cross the line
As the harebell clangs,
Take a bow
When the dawn comes up,
Proudly hold
The Acorn Cup,
Pat your mouse
And serve his dinner –
That's the way
To be a WINNER.

Clare Bevan

If You Hear . . .
(A poem murmured in Clare's ear)

If you think you hear a rustle
In the grasses by your door,
If you spot a tiny footprint
In the dust upon your floor,
If you see a baby sleeping
In the petals of a rose,
If you peer inside a mouse hole
And a lantern softly glows,
If your tooth, so small and precious
Is collected in the night,
Then perhaps you'll find the doorway
To the magic Land of Light.

Clare Bevan

The Fairy Rule Book
(This little book was tucked inside Clare's pencil box.)

1. Do not tease the Badger.
   (She will bite you.)
2. Do not hunt the Fieldmouse.
   (He will fight you.)
3. Never tickle Magpies.
   (They will snatch you.)
4. Never talk to Humans.
   (They will catch you.)

5. Always dance by Moonlight.
(It will glisten.)
6. Always trust the Barn Owl.
(She will listen.)
7. Wrap your wand in Starshine.
(It will shimmer.)
8. Treat your Glow-Worm kindly.
(It will glimmer.)
9. Clean your Magic Mirror.
(It will guide you.)
10. Wear your Cloak of Shadows.
(It will hide you.)
11. Read your Secret Spell Book.
(Read it nightly.)
12. Cast your Charms with Joy.
(And cast them lightly.)

IF YOU KEEP THESE FAIRY RULES
YOU'LL SPARKLE BRIGHTLY.

Clare Bevan

Ten Things a Real Princess Can Do
(This little list was found under Clare's feather bed.)

1. She can grow her hair as long (and as strong) as a ladder.
2. She can sleep for a hundred years without ever sneezing.
3. She can feel a single, tiny pea under a mountain of feathers.

4. She can find the only spinning wheel in the whole castle.
5. She can always spot a REAL prince, even if his clothes are torn by thorns or scorched by grumpy dragons.
6. She can turn a frog into a handsome prince, although he may have rather large feet.
7. She can dance until midnight in shiny, glass slippers (which is harder than you may think).
8. She can sew bundles of stinging nettles into soft, green shirts.
9. She can talk to her magic mirror (although she doesn't always believe what it says).
10. She can make her Ugly Sisters faint with surprise (but still remember to invite them to her wedding).

Clare Bevan

A Few Frightening Things
(Clare found this poem in the bucket of a haunted well.)

These are the things a Princess fears . . .

Broken mirrors,
Dragon tears,
Poisoned apples,
Wicked wands,
Slimy frogs
In slimy ponds,
Rusty keys
For creaky locks,

144

Stinging nettles,
Silent clocks,
Sharpened combs
By haunted wells,
Spinning wheels
And cruel spells,
Sleeping for
A hundred years . . .

These are the things a Princess fears.

Clare Bevan

What the Sleeping Beauty Dreamed
(Clare found this poem tangled inside a spider's web.)

She dreamed of rooms where danger spins,
She dreamed of guards with sleepy grins.

She dreamed of time that ticked and flew,
She dreamed of thorns that thickly grew.

She dreamed of hopes that drift and fade,
She dreamed of princes. Lost. Afraid.

She dreamed of someone handsome, who
Could beat the brambles, battle through
And weave his way past cobwebs too.

She woke – and found that dreams come true.

Clare Bevan

Mermaid School

(A crowd of little fishes is called a school. So what is a crowd of little mermaids called? Perhaps it is a SPLASH!)

What do mermaids learn at school?

How to sing beside a pool.
How to catch a flying fish.
How to grant an earth-child's wish.
How to chime a ship's old bell.
How to curl inside a shell.
How to win a sea-horse race.
How to swoop and dive and chase
Faster than the dolphin teams.
How to swim the silver beams
Of the small and misty moon.
How to play a magic tune.
How to tame a hungry shark.
How to find (when nights grow dark)
Hidden caves where treasures lie.
How to read a cloudy sky.
How to make a pearly ring.
How to mend a seabird's wing.
How to use a golden comb.
How to balance on the foam.
How to greet a friendly whale.
How to spin upon your tail.
How to twist and leap and turn . . .

This is what the mermaids learn.

Clare Bevan

The Mermaid Rap
(Mermaids say this poem to the beat of a turtle's flipper.)

I like whirlpools,
I'm the twirliest.

I like seaweed,
I'm the swirliest.

I like moonlight,
I'm the sleepiest.

I like whale songs,
I'm the weepiest.

I like clownfish,
I'm the funniest.

I like blue skies,
I'm the sunniest.

I like sea caves,
I'm the gloomiest.

I like storm winds,
I'm the zoomiest.

I like lobsters,
I'm the snappiest.

I like seasides –
I'm the HAPPIEST!

Clare Bevan

Shimmer, Glimmer
*(You can sing this poem to the tune of
'Twinkle, Twinkle, Little Star'.)*

Shimmer, glimmer, mermaid tails
With your gold and silver scales
How you sparkle, how you spin
While the little fishes grin.
Magic mermaids in the sea
Sing a sunny spell for me.

Clare Bevan

My Feelings and I

Just Doing

Your legs know how to walk
Your eyes know how to cry
Your mouth knows how to talk
Your heart knows how to fly.

Stephen Bowkett

Samantha Is Sobbing

Samantha is sobbing
By the playground wall
But why she should be sobbing
No one knows at all.

The sun shines brightly
The sky is blue
But Samantha is sobbing
Oh what shall we do?

Take her to Granny
Who lives down Comfort Lane
Once she gets to Granny's house
She'll never sob again.

She'll kiss her on the topknot
And treat her like a queen
Feed her new potatoes
Beans and margarine.

Gareth Owen

Shadow Collector

On summer afternoons
      sometimes evenings
I collect shadows . . .
      mainly people
      but sometimes cats and dogs.
I store them away
nice and flat
carefully ironed
between sheets of softest paper,
      free from light
      and prowling shadow thieves.
I collect my shadows from walls and pavements
      playground spaces
      beaches
      streets
      and gloomy places . . .
Old folk shadows
young and poor
teachers' shadows
(classroom floors).

But one is special
It's big.
It's tall.
And I found it on a palace wall.

Peter Dixon

Hiding

Behind this tree
You can't see me,
I've made myself thin
So I can fit in.

I'm as still as a photograph,
As quiet as a blink,
I won't sniff or laugh
Just quietly think.

Behind this tree
You can't see me,
I've made myself thin
So I can fit in.

Coral Rumble

The Cheer-up Song

No one likes a boaster
And I'm not one to boast,
But everyone who knows me knows
That I'm the most.

I'm the most attractive, I'm
The Media Superstar,
One hundred per cent in-tell-i-gent
And pop-u-lar.

All my jokes are funny.
Every one's a laugh.
Madonna pays me money for
My au-to-graph.

For I'm the snake's pyjamas, I'm
The bumble-bee's patella,
I'm a juicesome peach at a picnic on the beach, I'm
The rainmaker's umbrella.

Yes I'm the death-by-chocolate, I'm
The curried beans on toast,
And everyone who knows me knows that
I'm the most.

Tee-rr-eye-double-eff-eye-see
Triffic! TRIFFIC! TRIFFIC!
Yes it's me! ME! MEEE!

John Whitworth

A Big Surprise

For my presents, I said I'd like
Computer games,
A mountain bike,
An electric train
Or a model plane
But most of all
I'd like a bike.

I opened my presents
And what did I find there?
A hand knitted hat
And a squeaky bear,
More underpants from my aunts
And socks (grey, one pair).

I said 'thank you' nicely,
I tried to smile
But what was I thinking
All the while?
I was thinking
I wanted computer games,
A mountain bike,
An electric train
Or a model plane
But most of all
I'd have liked
A bike.

'There's just one last thing to unwrap,' they said.
'It's a big surprise
we've kept it in the shed.
It's special, it comes with love
From the lot of us . . .'

Now I'm the only kid in school
With my own hippopotamus.

Michaela Morgan

The Cupboard

I know a little cupboard,
With a teeny tiny key,
And there's a jar of Lollipops
For me, me, me.

It has a little shelf, my dear,
As dark as dark can be,
And there's a dish of Banbury Cakes
For me, me, me

I have a small fat grandmamma
With a very slippery knee,
And she's Keeper of the Cupboard
With the key, key, key.

And when I'm very good, my dear,
As good as good can be
There's Banbury Cakes, and Lollipops
For me, me, me.

Walter de la Mare

Pies

I spied a pie through the baker's door
And then I spied a whole lot more

Apple pie with crusty topping
Rabbit pie that won't stop hopping
Mince pie hot on Christmas Day
Pigeon pie that flies away
Cottage pie with bricks and mortar
Octopi found underwater
Butcher's pie with steak and kidney
Witch's pie with Kate and Sidney
Shepherd's pie with spuds and carrots
Pirate's pie with squawking parrots
Blackbird pie begins to sing
Eel pie keeps on wriggling
Custard pie that someone throws
Mud pie oozing through your toes
Fish pie swimming in the sea
Cherry pie – the one for me!

I spied a pie through the baker's door
A spider pie? Are you really sure?

Paul Bright

Noises in the Night

What's that scratching
at the window-pane?
Who's that knocking
again and again?
What's that creeping
across the floor?
And who's that tapping
at my bedroom door?

What's that creaking
beneath my bed?
Who's that walking
with a slow slow tread?
What's that whirring
in the air?
And who's that coming
up the squeaky stair?

I lie in bed
and I'm wide awake.
The noises make me
shiver and shake.
But soon all's quiet
and the dark is deep
so I close my eyes
and fall a . . .

Wes Magee

I Hated Everyone Today

I hated everyone today.
I took a boat and sailed away,
I found an island in the sea
And there was nobody but me;
It had a little wooden hut,
A palm tree and a coconut.

I walked upon the silver shore,
I met a red and blue macaw.
The tales he told of pirates bold,
Of brigantines and Spanish gold,
Of Captain Blood and Captain Kidd
And all the dreadful deeds they did!

They plundered, pillaged, smoked and drank,
They made their prisoners walk the plank –
You reach the end and then you drop;
It makes a horrid kind of plop.
The seas around for miles and miles
Were thick with happy crocodiles.

At night beneath the tropic moon
We swam across the lost lagoon
Where seals and phosphorescent fish
Shimmered like a Christmas wish.
I did exactly as I chose
And nobody got up my nose.

John Whitworth

Happy Poem

Happy as a rainbow
happy as a bee
happy as a dolphin
splashing in the sea

Happy as bare feet
running on the beach
happy as a sunflower
happy as a peach

Happy as a poppy
happy as a spoon
dripping with honey
happy as June

Happy as a banjo
plucking on a tune
happy as a Sunday
lazy afternoon

Happy as a memory
shared by two
happy as me . . .
when I'm with you

James Carter

A Smile

Smiling is infectious,
You catch it like the flu.
When someone smiled at me today
I started smiling too.

I passed around the corner
And someone saw my grin.
When he smiled, I realized
I'd passed it on to him.

I thought about my smile and then
I realized its worth.
A single smile like mine could travel
Right around the earth.

If you feel a smile begin
Don't leave it undetected.
Let's start an epidemic quick
And get the world infected.

Jez Alborough

162

Postcard

I didn't want to come to Spain,
But now I'm really glad I came.

The weather here is always fine.
Skies are blue here all the time.

I love the sand, the sea and sun.
I'm having lots and lots of fun.

Yesterday I had the chance
to learn to do a Spanish dance.

I'm learning to speak Spanish too.
'Como está?' means 'How are you?'

I didn't want to come to Spain,
but now I hope I'll come again!

Adios!

Tony Langham

Nativity

Oh Miss, I don't want to be Joseph,
Miss, I really don't want to be him,
With a cloak of bright red and a towel on my head
And a cottonwool beard on my chin.

Oh Miss, please don't make me a shepherd.
I just won't be able to sleep.
I'll go weak at the knees and wool makes me sneeze
And I really am frightened of sheep.

Oh Miss, I just can't be the landlord,
Who says there's no room in the inn.
I'll get in a fright when it comes to the night
And I know that I'll let Mary in.

Oh Miss, you're not serious – an angel?
Can't Peter take that part instead?
I'll look such a clown in a white silky gown,
And a halo stuck up on me head.

Oh Miss, I am not being a camel!
Or cow or an ox or an ass!
I'll look quite absurd and I won't say a word,
And all of the audience will laugh.

Oh Miss, I'd rather not be a Wise Man,
Who brings precious gifts from afar.
But the part right for me, and I hope you'll agree,
In this play – can I be the star?

Gervase Phinn

Moving Away

My best friend's leaving school today,
she's moving somewhere new.
Her house is on the market,
her brother's going too. . .

I saw the lorry loading
   her toys
   her coat
   her hat . . .
   her bike
   and books
   and bedclothes
   her hamster and her cat.

She said –
   she'd come and see me,
I said –
   I'd go and see her,
but I don't like these changes
   I liked things as they were.

Peter Dixon

My Friend

my friend is
like bark
rounding a tree

he warms
like sun
on a winter day

he cools
like water
in the hot noon

his voice
is ready
as a spring bird

he is
my friend
and I
am his

Emily Hearn

Mirror Friends

When we look in the mirror,
Me and my friend,
I am brown and she is white.
When we look in the mirror,
Me and my friend,
My hair is dark and hers is light.

And my eyes are black as a raven's wing,
And hers are as blue as a sapphire ring.
She likes chips
And I like rice,
She likes ketchup
And I like spice.

But when we look in the mirror,
Me and my friend
We feel we are the same as same can be,
Though I am brown and she is white,
We could be sisters,
She and me.

Jamila Gavin

What I'd Do for My Best Friend

I have a friend. Her name is Fleur,
And I'd do anything for her.

If my friend Fleur was kept in late,
I'd wait for her by the snicket gate.

If my friend Fleur slipped down a drain,
I'd try and pull her out again.

If she was down a deep dark hole,
I'd fish her out with a great long pole.

If my friend Fleur was put in jail,
I'd pay a million pounds in bail.

If she fell off our garden wall,
I'd compliment her on her fall.

But if she was really scared at night,
I'd let her borrow my nightlight.

If my friend Fleur was up the creek,
I'd go and see her every week.

If my best friend was in a stew,
I wouldn't eat it. Well, would you?

If Fleur was eaten by a lion,
I don't think I would ever stop cryin'.

If she was eaten by a gerbil,
I wouldn't laugh. (Though I might burble.)

'Cos she's my friend, my very best friend.
That's all I've got to say.

The End

Gerard Benson

Last Lick

Sue and me walk home from school together every day,
We play 'teacher' and 'hide an' seek', and 'tag' along the
   way,
But the best game is the one we always leave until the end.
Till just before we reach her gate, right beside the double
   bend.
Sue always get me first, but she won't get me today.
So as she reaching out her hand, I jump out of the way,
Then before she know, I stretch out my hand and touch her
   quick,
And as I racing down the road, I holler out 'LAST LICK!'

Valerie Bloom

Lion

I have a box
in which I keep
a shoulder I may cry on,
I lift the lid
and there inside's
a large and lovely lion.

My lion is wild
with glorious mane,
a pounce in every paw,
I have to keep
him in a box
for fear that he may roar.

The box is small,
you'd hardly think
the King of Beasts would fit,
I only keep
my lion there
by training him to sit.

From time to time
I lift the lid
to hear my lion purr,
and gently stroke
my fingers through
his soft and friendly fur.

I have a box
in which I keep
a secret to rely on,
so carefully close
the lid upon
my large and lovely lion.

Celia Warren

Orange Shoes

I saw a girl today wearing orange shoes
she had blonde hair in pig-tails, and these orange shoes –
such a jumped-up orange they were,
it seemed as though she danced on marigolds.

I bet the pavement was glad.

Anne Bell

Inside

Now
you
may think
I'm walking tall
I'm talking big
I've got it all –
but here inside
I'm ever so shy
I sometimes cry
I'm curled in a ball
I'm no feet small

no	I'm
not	big
not	tall
at	all

James Carter

The Fisherman's Wife

When I am alone,
The wind in the pine-trees
Is like the shuffling of waves
Upon the wooden sides of a boat.

Amy Lowell

172

These Are the Hands

These are the hands that wave
These are the hands that clap
These are the hands that pray
These are the hands that tap

These are the hands that grip
These are the hands that write
These are the hands that paint
These are the hands that fight

These are the hands that hug
These are the hands that squeeze
These are the hands that point
These are the hands that tease

These are the hands that fix
These are the hands that mend
These are the hands that give
These are the hands that lend

These are the hands that take
These are the hands that poke
These are the hands that heal
These are the hands that stroke

These are the hands that hold
These are the hands that love
These are the hands of mine
That fit me like a glove

Paul Cookson

Sounds

Crunching ginger biscuits
is like hearing soldiers tread
marching over gravel
on the inside of your head.

Chewing a marshmallow
is nowhere near as loud.
It's the smaller, sweet equivalent
of swallowing a cloud.

Stewart Henderson

Wings

If I had wings I would touch
the frail fingertips of clouds.

If I had wings I would taste
a chunk of the sun, as hot as peppered curry.

174

If I had wings I would listen
to the clouds' soft breath.

If I had wings I would smell
the scent of fresh raindrops.

If I had wings I would gaze
at the people who cling to the earth's crust.

If I had wings I would dream
of swimming the deserts
 And walking the seas.

Pie Corbett

In This Room

With my little eye
I can see the whiteboard
covered with writing.

With my little eye
I can see a painting of a unicorn
flying over the forest.

With my little ear
I can hear the heating rumble
and the sound of someone chewing a sweet.

With my little ear
I can hear teachers talking
but no one is listening!

With my little hand
I can touch the cold glass of milk
and feel its smooth skin.

Pie Corbett

Topsy Turvy

This morning the world
Was topsy turvy.

The cars started talking
to the red buses.

The lamp post bent down
and tickled a dustbin.

The houses yawned
and fell fast asleep.

The chairs giggled
and the table sneezed.

The light began to sing
a nursery rhyme.

The floor wished
that everyone would tiptoe.

The door closed shut
and said, 'Goodnight!'

Pie Corbett

I Wonder Why

I wonder why the sky is blue
And why this rose is red,
And why I have to wash my face
And go so soon to bed.

Jane Mann

Paint

I should like to paint
the eye of a raindrop
the foot of a thunderclap
the heart of a cloud

the roving eye of dew
clawed foot of lightning
the elastic heart of cumulus

paint
a mascara-ed eye
a sultry heart
a silken foot

then
black cloud
forked lightning
a splintered raindrop

a squall of rain
wet hair on a brow
a dubious eye

*A finger of rain walking across a sodden field to
a fringe of wood where a majestic tree is falling*

Brian Morse

The Animal World

Noisy Garden

If tiger lilies and dandelions growled,
And cowslips mooed, and dog roses howled,
And snapdragons roared and catmint miaowed,
My garden would be extremely loud.

Julia Donaldson

'Quack!' Said the Billy-goat

'Quack!' said the billy-goat.
  'Oink!' said the hen.
'Miaow!' said the little chick
  Running in the pen.

'Hobble-gobble!' said the dog.
  'Cluck!' said the sow.
'Tu-whit tu-whoo!' the donkey said.
  'Baa!' said the cow.

'Hee-haw!' the turkey cried.
  The duck began to moo.
All at once the sheep went,
  'Cock-a-doodle-doo!'

The owl coughed and cleared his throat
 And he began to bleat.
'Bow-wow!' said the cock
 Swimming in the leat.

'Cheep-cheep!' said the cat
 As she began to fly.
'Farmer's been and laid an egg –
 That's the reason why.'

       Charles Causley

The Day the Zoo Escaped

The day the zoo escaped . . .

 the zebras zipped out quickly,
 the snakes slid out slickly,

  the lions marched out proudly,
  the hyenas laughed out loudly,

   the mice skipped out lightly,
   the parrots flew out brightly,

    but the hippopotamus,
    stubbornly,

     just stayed where it was.

Michaela Morgan and Sue Palmer

Buzz Buzz

Bees on your fingers,
Bees on your toes,
Bees in your ear-holes
And bees up your nose.

Bees on your tongue-tip,
Bees between your teeth,
Bees, bees on top of bees
And bees underneath.

Bees in your toothpaste,
Bees on your brush,
Bees going **BOOM BOOM!**
And bees going hush.

Bees on your Weetabix,
Bees wearing boots,
Bees wearing T-shirts
And bees in best suits.

Bees up the chimney,
Bees down the drain,
Bees bumping into bees,
Oh not bees again!

Bees in your school-bag,
Bees in your bed,
Bees live a buzzy life
Then
        drop
                down
                        dead.

John Mole

The Bee's Story

'Buzz! Buzz!' said the bee.
'If you listen to the flea
Or the pretty butterfly
Or the spotty ladybird
You would never ever know
That they're flitter flying by
And you'll maybe wonder why
I buzz.
Now mosquitoes have a whine
And a whine is very fine
And the beetles sometimes click
And the death watch beetles tick
But a bee will always buzz.
It's what we does.
we **BUZZ!**

And it may be 'cos we're busy
Busy buzzing to and fro
And we buzz around for hours
As we pollinate the flowers
(Don't you think, if we're so busy,
We should **BIZZ** instead of
BUZZ?
Maybe someone couldn't spell –
Who can tell?)
And we're busy being **BUZZY**
Every day
So when you hear somebody say
"What a busy little bee"
Think of me.
Buzz buzz.
It's what we does.'

Vivian French

Greedy Dog

This dog will eat anything.

Apple cores and bacon fat,
Milk you poured out for the cat.
He likes the string that ties the roast
And relishes hot buttered toast.
Hide your chocolates! He's a thief,

He'll even eat your handkerchief.
And if you don't like sudden shocks,
Carefully conceal your socks.
Leave some soup without a lid,
And you'll wish you never did.
When you think he must be full,
You find him gobbling bits of wool,
Orange peel or paper bags,
Dusters and old cleaning rags.

This dog will eat anything,
Except for mushrooms and cucumber.

Now what is wrong with those, I wonder?

James Hurley

Shaggy Dogs

Two sheepdogs in a field
Looked up and wondered why
A great big flock of woolly sheep
Was cluttering up the sky.

The sheepdogs growled and leaped
And climbed the slopes of air,
Yapping, snarling, nipping, snapping,
Scattering sheep everywhere.

And when the sky was clear again
They hurried home together
Back to their field to sunbathe
In the warm blue weather.

Richard Edwards

The Guide Dog's Story

'Young Catherine has lost her sight,
and now her world is dark as night.

I am well trained. I am her guide.
Together we walk side by side.

Young Catherine has lost her sight.
Each sunny day is black as night.

I let her know where danger lies.
I am the blind girl's seeing eyes.'

Wes Magee

We Saw a Hare

Where? Where?
There! There!
The shy hare,
not a care,
up at dawn
stitching corn
with her pair
of sharp ears!!
The hare hears,
as she bobs along,
sunlight's song.
Sewing; glowing.
Where's she going?
GONE!!

Pie Corbett

Our Cats

Our cats stay out all night
. . . moonlighting.
You should hear them spitting and
  fighting.

At breakfast-time they come in
. . . purring,
and curl on chairs, no hint of
  stirring.

Then when it's dark they're off
. . . exploring
while thunder growls and gales are
    roaring.

When we're tucked up in bed
. . . fast-sleeping
they're out there in the darkness,
    creeping.

Wes Magee

Cat

You need your Cat.
When you slump down
All tired and flat
With too much town

With too many lifts
Too many floors
Too many neon-lit
Corridors

Too many people
Telling you what
You just must do
And what you must not

189

With too much headache
Video glow
Too many answers
You never will know

Then stroke the Cat
That warms your knee
You'll find her purr
Is a battery

For into your hands
Will flow the powers
Of the beasts who ignore
These ways of ours

And you'll be refreshed
Through the Cat on your lap
With a Leopard's yawn
And a Tiger's nap.

Ted Hughes

You Are

The Oxo in the gravy,
the Bisto in my stew,
the custard on my pudding,
the window with a view.

You're the pressie in the cracker,
you're the apple in the pie,
the answer to the question,
the twinkle in the eye.

You're the magic in the secret,
my firework in the night,
my sunshine in the morning,
the sum that's always right.

You are neither rich nor famous
but to me you are the best –
you're the head upon my pillow
and the paw upon my chest.

Peter Dixon

The Owl and the Pussy-cat

The Owl and the Pussy-cat went to sea
  In a beautiful pea-green boat,
They took some honey, and plenty of money,
  Wrapped up in a five-pound note.
The Owl looked up to the stars above,
  And sang to a small guitar,
'O lovely Pussy! O Pussy, my love,
    What a beautiful Pussy you are,
      You are,
      You are!
    What a beautiful Pussy you are!'

Pussy said to the Owl, 'You elegant fowl!
   How charmingly sweet you sing!
O let us be married! too long we have tarried:
   But what shall we do for a ring?'
They sailed away, for a year and a day,
   To the land where the Bong-tree grows
And there in a wood a Piggy-wig stood
   With a ring at the end of his nose,
     His nose,
     His nose,
   With a ring at the end of his nose.

'Dear Pig, are you willing to sell for one shilling
   Your ring?' Said the Piggy, 'I will.'
So they took it away, and were married next day
   By the Turkey who lives on the hill.
They dined on mince, and slices of quince,
   Which they ate with a runcible spoon;
And hand in hand, on the edge of the sand,
   They danced by the light of the moon,
     The moon,
     The moon,
   They danced by the light of the moon.

Edward Lear

Big Fat Budgie

I'm a big fat budgie,
I don't do a lot.
Might park on my perch.
Might peek at my mirror.
Might ring my bell.
Might peer through the bars of my fat budgie cell.
Might say 'Who's a pretty boy then?'
Might not.
I'm a big fat budgie.
I don't do a lot.

Michaela Morgan

First Fox

A big fox stands in the spring grass,
Glossy in the sun, chestnut bright,
Plumb centre of the open meadow, a leaf
From a picturebook.

Forepaws delicately nervous,
Thick brush on the grass
He rakes the air for the scent
Of the train rushing by.

My first fox,
Wiped from my eye,
In a moment of train-time.

Pamela Gillilan

Guess What I Am

I am a fly-by-night,
Silent in flight,
Scanning the fields,
Waiting to sweep by.

You might see me at rest
On a post, eyes clamped
Tight as shells –

Like a shadow
I'll come, calling
In the dark –
Who? Who? Who?

But the night
Does not answer back.
The bushes hold their breath.
The fields are locked up
So I drift by. . .

Till in the headlamps
You might spot me
Like a ghost of the dead
Flapping overhead . . .

Pie Corbett

The Barn Owl

High up on the rafters
Something white
Sleeps in the shadows
Waiting for the night.

High up from the rafters
Something flies,
With silent wings
And big round eyes.

Richard James

Cuckoo

The Cuckoo's the crookedest, wickedest bird.
His song has two notes, but only one word.

He says to the Linnet: 'Your eggs look so ill!
Now I am the Doctor, and here is my pill.'

195

Within that pill, the Cuckoo-child
Crouches hidden, wicked and wild.

He bursts his shell, and with weightlifter's legs
He flings from the nest the Linnet's eggs.

Then bawls to the Linnet: 'Look at me, Mam!
How quickly I've grown, and how hungry I am!'

She thinks he is hers, she is silly with joy.
She wears herself bare for the horrible boy.

Till one day he burps, with a pitiless laugh,
'I've had enough of this awful Caf!'

And away he whirls, to Cuckooland,
And leaves her to weep with a worm in her hand.

Ted Hughes

Milking Time

Five o'clock in the morning
cows cross the dark yard
like white patches of jigsaw,
their hot breath making misty ghosts
in the crisp air.

Gina Douthwaite

Bears Don't Like Bananas

Monkeys like to play the drums,
   badgers wear bandannas.
Tigers like to tickle toes
   but bears don't like bananas.

A crocodile can juggle buns
   on visits to his nana's.
Seagulls like to dance and sing
   but bears don't like bananas.

Rats and mice can somersault
   and do gymnastics with iguanas.
Weasels like to wiggle legs
   but bears don't like bananas.

A porcupine likes drinking tea,
   and cheering at gymkhanas.
A ladybird likes eating pies
   but bears don't like bananas.

John Rice

The Small Brown Bear

The small brown bear
fishes
with stony paws

eating ice salmon
all waterfall slippery
till his teeth ache.

Michael Baldwin

Arctic Vixen

The snowfox
the winter fox

is the colour
of bushy snow

her breath
like a white brush

and her eye
rusty.

Michael Baldwin

Elephant Walking

We're swaying through the jungle
Dizzy with the heat,
Searching for a water-hole
To cool our heavy feet.

Trample on the grasses;
Then stop and breathe the scent
Of flower and leaf – and tiger!
And we watch the way he went.

Then on again we stumble,
Searching for a drink;
We find a spilling river,
And into it we sink.

Clive Sansom

The Corn Scratch Kwa Kwa Hen and the Fox

And the Corn Scratch Kwa Kwa Hen
Heard the grumbling rumbling belly
Of the Slink Back Brush Tail Fox
A whole field away.

And she said to her sisters in the henhouse,
'Sisters, that Slink Back Brush Tail Fox
Will come and here's what we must do,'
And she whispered in their sharp sharp ears, 'kwa kwa.'

And when that Slink Back Brush Tail Fox
Came over the field at night,
She heard his paw slide on a leaf,
And the Corn Scratch Kwa Kwa Hen and her sisters
Opened their beaks and –

'KWA!'
The moon jumped
And the Chooky Chook Chicks
Hid under the straw and giggled,
It was the **LOUDEST KWA** in the world.

And the Log Dog and the Scat Cat
And the Brat Rat and the House Mouse
And the Don't Harm Her Farmer
And his Life Wife and their Shorter Daughter
And their One Son came running,

On their slip slop, flip flop,
Scatter clatter, slick flick, tickly feet
And they opened their mouths and shouted –

'FOX!'
And it was the **LOUDEST NAME** in the world.
And the Slink Back Brush Tail Fox
Ran over the fields and far away
And hid in a hole with his grumbling rumbling belly.

And the Corn Scratch Kwa Kwa Hen
Tucked the Chooky Chook Chicks under her feathers
And said 'kwa,'
And it was the softest kwa in the world.

Julie Holder

The Crow and the Fox

Fox on the ground, crow in the trees.
Fox feeling hungry, crow has some cheese.
Fox licks his lips. 'Good morning, hello.
How do you do, you beautiful crow?'

Hush, silly bird, don't open your beak –
You'll lose that cheese if you speak.

Fox tries again: 'Beautiful day,
Don't you agree? What do you say?
Elegant bird with feathers so sleek,
Can you be dumb? Why don't you speak?'

Hush, silly bird, don't open your beak –
You'll lose that cheese if you speak.

'Your wings and your tail are glossy and dark.
Your eyes are like diamonds, your voice like a lark.
Sing for me now! Oh how I long
To hear just one note – won't you sing me a song?'

Hush, silly bird, don't open your beak –
You'll lose that cheese if you speak.

Crow feeling good, puffing with pride,
Eyes shining brightly, head on one side.
Opens her beak, lets out a sound – CAAAAAAGH!
Down falls the cheese to fox on the ground.

Hush, silly bird, why did you croak?
You lost that cheese when you spoke.

Fox on the ground, crow in the trees,
Crow feeling hungry, fox has the cheese.

Julia Donaldson

The Stork and the Fox

A stork was stretching her legs one day
When a sly old fox came slinking her way.
'Good morning, Stork. I have something to say:
An extra-special request.
I was stirring some soup when I thought of you.
Oh do come and dine with me, Stork, yes do!
Dinner is much better fun with two,
So be my guest.'

When the fox had sounded the dinner gong
The stork found out there was something wrong
For the plate was flat and her beak was long
And not a drop did she taste.
Said the fox, 'You're slimming, it's plain to see,
Or you ate too much for your lunch, maybe.
Just take it easy and leave it to me
For I can't stand waste.'

The fox was brushing his tail next day
When the tall white stork came strutting his way.
'Good morning, Fox. I have something to say:
An extra-special request.
Tonight for supper I dearly wish
That you'd come and join me to eat a dish
Of every kind of delicious fish.
Yes, be my guest.'

As the fox sat down to the meal, he thought,
'There may be a catch but I won't be caught,'
But the jug was deep and his tongue was short
And not a scrap did he taste.
Said the stork, 'You've lost your good appetite
So I'm sure you won't mind if I have the last bite
For I seem to remember you told me last night
That you can't stand waste.'

Julia Donaldson

The Tortoise and the Hare

The hare was the handsomest hare in the world
With a white fluffy bobtail and whiskers that curled.
He lived in a field and his favourite sport was
Leapfrogging over the back of the tortoise.
The hare went a-loping, a-lolloping, a-leaping.
The tortoise went crawling, a-creaking, a-creeping.

The hare claimed that no one was faster than he.
He asked all the animals, 'Who'll race with me?'
The tortoise said, 'I will!' The hare roared with laughter.
'Race with a tortoise? Why, what could be dafter?
I'll go a-loping, a-lolloping, a-leaping.
You'll go a-crawling, a-creaking, a-creeping.'

They mapped out a course and they fixed a day.
It's one two three go! and the hare is away,
Whisking his bobtail and frisking and gambolling.
Way back behind him the tortoise is ambling.
The hare goes a-loping, a-lolloping, a-leaping.
The tortoise comes crawling, a-creaking, a-creeping.

The hare is halfway when he stretches and blinks.
I've nothing to lose if I snatch forty winks.'
His head drops, his eyes close, and soon he is slumbering.
Inching towards him the tortoise is lumbering.
The hare is a-snoring, a-snoozing, a-sleeping.
The tortoise comes crawling, a-creaking, a-creeping.

The hare wakes and starts: is it real or a ghost?
The tortoise is nearing the finishing post.
The hare helter-skelters but just doesn't do it.
Slowcoach the tortoise has beaten him to it.
The hare lost a-snoring, a-snoozing, a-sleeping.
The tortoise won crawling, a-creaking, a-creeping.

Julia Donaldson

The Mouse and the Lion

In the hottest sun of the longest day
A lion lay down for a doze.
A little brown mouse pattered out to play.
He danced on the whiskery nose.
Pit-a-pat, pit-a-pat, pit-a-pat, pit-a-pat,
He danced on the whiskery nose.

The lion awoke with a sneeze, 'A-choo!'
He picked up the mouse in his paw.
'And who may I venture to ask are you?'
He said with a terrible roar.
Grr, grrr, grrrrr, GRRRRRR,
He said with a terrible roar.

'I'll save your life if you'll let me go.'
The mouse's voice shook as he spoke.
The lion laughed loudly, 'Oh ho ho ho.
I'll let you go free for your joke.'
Oho, oho, ohohohoho,
I'll let you go free for your joke.

As chance would have it, the following week
The lion was caught in a net
When all of a sudden he heard a squeak:
'Well met, noble lion, well met.'
Squeak, squeak, squeak, squeak,
Well met, noble lion, well met.

The little mouse nibbled and gnawed and bit
Till the lion was finally free.
'It's nothing, dear lion, don't mention it:
I'm repaying your kindness to me.'
Nibbly, nibbly, nibbly, nibble,
Repaying your kindness to me.

'For one of the lessons which mice must learn
From their whiskery father and mother
Is the famous old saying that one good turn
Always deserves another.'
Pit-a-pat, grrr, ohoho, squeak!
Always deserves another.

Julia Donaldson

Hippopotamus Dancing

In the hippo house
at the city zoo,
hippos are moving
to the boogaloo,
big hippos shuffle,
little hippos trot,
everyone giving it
all they've got . . .

Hip-hippo, hippopotamus dancing,
hip-hippo, hippopotamus dancing.

Every hippo keeping fit,
fighting the flab
doing their bit,
weight training one week,
aerobics another,
tiny hippopotami
move with their mothers . . .

Hip-hippo, hippopotamus dancing,
hip-hippo, hippopotamus dancing.

Hippos in tutus,
hippos in vests,
baby hippos
doing their best
to keep clear of Dad
as he stumbles around,
causing commotion
shaking the ground . . .

Hip-hippo, hippopotamus dancing,
hip-hippo, hippopotamus dancing.

Brian Moses

Ollie the Wallaby

Ollie the Wallaby
cannot fly.

He doesn't
know *why* –
and neither
do I.

Katherine Gallagher

Kangaroos

Kangaroos are hoppity
Kangaroos are fun,
If you want to catch a Kangaroo
You'll really have to run.

Kangaroos are jumpy
Bounding over the plain,
You can't hold down a Kangaroo
'Cause he'll bounce up again!

Kangaroos are tough guys
They can box as well,
If a Kangaroo should hit you
Your head rings like a bell!

Kangaroo Mums are kindly
For their young they have a pocket,
Where babies can feed and feel quite safe
While Mum takes off like a rocket!

John Cotton

I Wannabe a Wallaby

I wannabe a wallaby,
A wallaby that's true.
Don't wannabe a possum
A koala or a roo.

I wannago hop hopping
Anywhere I please.
Hopping without stopping
Through eucalyptus trees.

A wallaby, a wallaby
Is what I wannabe.
I'd swap my life to be one,
But a problem – I can see;

If I'm gonna be a wallaby
I shall have to go and see
If I can find a wallaby,
A very friendly wallaby,
Who would really, really, really . . .

Wannabe . . . ME!

David Whitehead

210

The Dinosaur's Dinner

Once a mighty dinosaur
Came to dine with me,
He gobbled up the curtains
And swallowed our settee.

He didn't seem to fancy
Onion soup with crusty bread,
He much preferred the flavour
Of our furniture instead.

He ate up all our dining-chairs
And carpets from the floor,
He polished off the table, then
He looked around for more.

The television disappeared
In one almighty gulp,
Wardrobes, beds and bathroom
He crunched into a pulp.

He really loved the greenhouse,
He liked the garden shed,
He started on the chimney-pots
But then my mother said:

'Your friends are always welcome
To drop in for a bite,
But really this one seems to have
A giant appetite.

You'd better take him somewhere else.
I'm sure I don't know where,
I only know this friend of yours
Needs more than we can spare!'

And suddenly I realized
I knew the very place,
And when I showed him where it was
You should have seen his face –

I don't think I've seen anyone
Enjoy a dinner more,
I watched him wander on his way,
A happy dinosaur!

The council did rebuild our school,
But that of course took time . . .
And all because a dinosaur
Came home with me to dine!

June Crebbin

Families and Other Folk

The Key

This is the key
this is the door
this is the rug
sat on the floor

This is the phone
out in the hall
this is our photo
up on the wall

This is the table
these are the chairs
see over here:
these are the stairs

This is the landing
this is the light
this is my room
I sleep here at night

This is my family
this is me
this is my home
this is the key

James Carter

Dad and Me

Up in his wardrobe, my dad has a very old baseball glove
That was his when he was a kid.
In my wardrobe, I have an old blanket called Softie
That was mine when I was very little.
Dad never uses his glove anymore
And I don't use Softie.
But Dad doesn't want to throw his glove away
And I don't want to throw away my blanket either.
We just want to keep them.
If you ask us why,
We say we don't know why, we just do.

Jeff Moss

Missing Important Things

I didn't go to school this week
I stayed at home with Dad.
I didn't do a worksheet
and I am really rather glad.
I didn't do the number work,
I didn't do my words,
I didn't learn my spellings
and I didn't read my page.
I didn't go to school, today –
we fixed the shed instead,

tied some flies and feathers
and dug the onion bed.
I saw the cat have kittens,
I climbed right up a tree,
mixed some sand and water
and held a bumblebee.
I didn't go to school all week
and I'm really not too sad –
I missed important lessons
and stayed at home with Dad.

Peter Dixon

My Dad's Amazing!

My Dad's AMAZING for he can:

make mountains out of molehills,
teach Granny to suck eggs,
make Mum's blood boil,
and then drive her up the wall.

My Dad's AMAZING for he also:

walks around with his head in the clouds,
has my sister eating out of his hand,
says he's got eyes in the back of his head
and can read me like a book.

BUT,
the most AMAZING thing of all is:

when he's caught someone red-handed
first he jumps down their throat
and then he bites their head off!

Ian Souter

Eddie and the Nappy

Eddie hates having his nappy done.
So I say all cheery,
'Time for your nappy, Eddie,'
and he says, all sad,
'No nappeee.'
And I say,
'Yes, nappy.'
So I have to run after him going,
'Nappy nappy nappy nappy . . .'

And he's got these little fat rubbery legs
that go round like wheels;
so away he runs
with a wicked grin on his face
screaming,
'Woooo woooo woooo.'

So I go running after him
shouting,
'Nappy nappy nappy,
I'll get you I'll get you . . .'
until I catch him.

Then I lift him up
lay him over my knees
to get his nappy off.

While I'm doing the pins
he gargles,
'Geereegreegeereegree,'
waving his podgy little legs in the air.
He thinks,
great. Time to kick Dad's chin.
And smack smack smack
on my chin.

When I've cleaned him up
it's time for the cream
You have to put cream on a baby's bum
or they get nappy rash.
But we leave the jar of cream
on the window-sill
where it gets all cold.
So I go,
'Time for the cream, Eddie.'
And he goes,
'No cream.'

So I say,
'Yeah, cream,'
and I blob it on
and he goes, 'Oooh.'
You imagine what that would feel like.
A great blob of cold cream.
It would be like
having an ice-lolly down your pants.

So then I put the nappy on
and away he goes on those little rubbery legs going,
'Woooo woooo woooo.'

Michael Rosen

Squeezes

We love to squeeze bananas,
We love to squeeze ripe plums,
And when they are feeling sad
We love to squeeze our mums.

Brian Patten

Love Me Mum

Love me
Even though I sulk for days.
Love me
Even when I answer back.
Love me
Even when I get in trouble.
Love me Mum
For I love you.

I love you
Even when I rant and rave.
I love you
Even when I'm in a mood.
I love you
Even when I'm nagging on.
I love you
For I'm your mum.

Brenda Williams

Calling Names

I call my brother
Waggle Ears, Banana Boots
And Nobble Nose.

He calls me Mop Head,
Turnip Top,
Potato Pie and Twinkle Toes.

I call him Weed,
He calls me Wimp
Then Mum comes in the door.

She calls us Double Trouble
Then we're both
Best friends once more.

Irene Rawnsley

Don't Be Such a Fusspot

Don't be such a fusspot,
an always-in-a-rushpot.

Don't be such a weepypot,
a sneak-to-mum-and-be-creepypot.

Don't be such a muddlepot,
a double-dose-of-troublepot.

Don't be such a wigglepot,
a sit-on-your-seat-don't-squigglepot.

Don't be such a muckypot,
a pick-up-slugs-and-be-yuckypot.

Don't be such a sleepypot,
a beneath-the-bedclothes-peepypot.

Don't be such a fiddlepot,
a mess-about-and-meddlepot.

Don't be such a bossypot,
a saucypot, a gigglepot.

Don't be such a lazypot,
a nigglepot, a slackpot.

And don't call me a crackpot . . .
Who do you think you are?

Brian Moses

I Don't Want an Avocado for an Uncle

I don't want an icicle for an auntie,
she might snap.

I don't want a tomato for an older brother,
he might go red in the face.

I don't want a candle for a gran,
she might melt.

I don't want a coffee bean for a cousin,
he might get swallowed from a cup.

I don't want a blister for a sister,
she might get sore.

I don't want an avocado for an uncle,
he might go squishy.

I don't want a carpet for a granddad,
he might be threadbare.

I don't want a plum for a mum,
she might get made into chutney.

I don't want a diamond for a dad
because he'd be the hardest man in the world.

Chrissie Gittins

Great-aunt Polly

Roly-poly, sugar-dusted
as a jam doughnut,
she wears round
wire-rimmed glasses
and her eyes shine
like wet pebbles.

She loves to gossip,
leans on the garden gate
toasting in the sunshine.
Her mouth is small,
painted red, pursed
as a ripe raspberry.

Great-aunt Polly
puts on a squashy hat
and walks to church
on Sundays. She
knows everyone, hands
round mints to suck.

Moira Andrew

Grandma

Grandma is teaching the trees to sing,
Building them giant harps,
Stringing their branches with long humming wires,
Painting their limbs with pictures of larks.

Grandma is teaching the cows to dance,
Sewing them evening gowns,
Sprinkling sequins along their black tails,
Waltzing them over the downs.

Grandma is showing the frogs how to fly
So high on the circus trapeze.
She swoops to the music of wild violins
Then gracefully hangs by her knees.

Jan Dean

Gran's Old Diary

I found my Gran's old diary,
it has a lock and key.
I found it in the attic,
when you explored with me.

My Gran wrote her old diary
many years ago.
She used the blackest ink
on pages white as snow.

And inside Gran's old diary
something caught my eye:
it was a tiny buttercup
pressed flat from years gone by.

Wes Magee

Granny Granny
Please Comb My Hair

Granny Granny please comb my hair
you always take your time
you always take such care

You put me on a cushion between your knees
you rub a little coconut oil
parting gentle as a breeze

Mummy Mummy
she's always in a hurry-hurry
rush
she pulls my hair
sometimes she tugs

227

But Granny
you have all the time
in the world
and when you're finished
you always turn my head and say
'Now who's a nice girl?'

Grace Nichols

Burying Moses

Moses was very old,
Ninety-eight, my grandpa said,
So we shouldn't cry too much
Now poor old Moses was dead.

Moses used to be black
But he slowly turned grey as a fog
And snuffled and wheezed and snored.
Moses was our old dog.

Each year that people live
Counts for a dog as seven.
'He was a good old boy,' said grandpa,
'He's sure to go to heaven.

'But first we must go and bury him
At the back of the garden shed,
So come and give me a hand;
We'll make him a deep warm bed.'

228

And so we lowered old Moses
Down in the hole grandpa dug,
And he huddled there in a bundle
Like a dusty old fireside rug.

Then we filled in the hole and patted
The soil down smooth and flat.
'I'll make him a cross,' said Grandpa.
'The least we can do is that.

'He'll be wagging his tail in heaven,
So you mustn't be upset . . .'
But grandpa's voice sounded croaky,
And I could see his old cheeks were wet.

Vernon Scannell

I Like to Stay Up

I like to stay up
and listen
when big people talking
jumbie* stories

I does feel
so tingly and excited
inside me

But when my mother say
'Girl, time for bed'

229

Then is when
I does feel a dread

Then is when
I does jump into me bed

Then is when
I does cover up
from me feet to me head

Then is when
I does wish I didn't listen
to no stupid jumbie story

Then is when I does wish I did read
me book instead

* *'Jumbie' is a Guyanese word for 'ghost'*

Grace Nichols

Silly Billy Banjo

Silly Billy Banjo plays his song,
high Billy Banjo, low Billy Banjo,
silly Billy Banjo plays his song,
high Billy, low Billy,
silly Billy Banjo.

Silly Billy Banjo plays his song,
quick Billy Banjo, s – l – o – w Billy Banjo,
silly Billy Banjo plays his song,
quick Billy, s – l – o – w Billy,
high Billy, low Billy,
silly Billy Banjo.

Silly Billy Banjo plays his song,
shhh Billy Banjo, **YO!** Billy Banjo,
silly Billy Banjo plays his song,
shhh Billy, **YO!** Billy,
quick Billy, s – l – o – w Billy,
high Billy, low Billy,
silly Billy Banjo.

Silly Billy Banjo plays his song,
STOP! Billy Banjo, GO! Billy Banjo,
silly Billy Banjo plays his song,
STOP! Billy, GO! Billy,
shhh Billy, **YO!** Billy,
quick Billy, s – l – o – w Billy,
high Billy, low Billy,
silly Billy Banjo.

High low high low
quick s – l – o – w quick s – l – o – w
shhh **YO!** shhh **YO!**   *(repeat three times,*
Stop! GO! Stop! GO!   *increasing speed)*

Silly Billy Banjo **stop!**
Silly Billy Banjo **stop! STOP! STOP!**

Nick Penny

231

Give Me a House

Give me a house, said Polly.
Give me land, said Hugh.
Give me the moon, said Sadie.
Give me the sun, said Sue.

Give me a horse, said Rollo.
Give me a hound, said Joe.
Give me fine linen, said Sarah.
Give me silk, said Flo.

Give me a mountain, said Kirsty.
Give me a valley, said Jim.
Give me a river, said Dodo.
Give me the sky, said Tim.

Give me the ocean, said Adam.
Give me a ship, said Hal.
Give me a kingdom, said Rory.
Give me a crown, said Sal.

Give me gold, said Peter.
Give me silver, said Paul.
Give me love, said Jenny,
Or nothing at all.

Charles Causley

Show & Tell

Amber showed a little shell
Bella told us how she fell
Carla went to see her nan
Dylan went to see West Ham
Erin did a ballet dance
Faron's daddy went to France
Georgia talked about her aunty
Hannah's going to have a party
Ian brought his football cards
Joey showed his model cars
Kieran told us he'd been naughty
Lauren counted up to forty
Maddy sang her favourite song
Noah's baby won't be long
Ollie went to Dylan's home
Paris said she used the phone
TariQ showed a paper swan
Ryan's brother's nearly 1
Sophie made a frog with clay
Tina's Nana came to stay
Una's learning how to swim
Vinny brought some acorns in

William laughed and told a joke
MaX put on his wizard's cloak
Yasmine said a funny rhyme
Zoe said she'd show next time

James Carter

Getting Back Home

Hang your hat on the peg
Rest up, rest up
Fling your coat on the bed
For you have travelled many miles to see me.

Put your feet on the bench
Rest up, rest up
Heave off your heavy boots
For you have come through winter days to see me.

Settle down by the fire
Rest up, rest up
Lean back and smile at me
For after all this time and travelling
Oh traveller, I'm glad to see you.

Jenny Joseph

The Natural World – Day Turning, Seasons Changing

Blessings

Bless the blue sky,
bright as a bride.
Bless the clear sea,
and creatures that hide.

Bless the deep sleep,
sweet with a dream.
Bless every flower
and the fresh stream.
Bless the sun's glow
and the plant's green.
Bless the proud earth,
the eagle's scream.

Bless the Scots thistle
and the slithery snake.
Bless the smooth fish
that swims in the lake.

Bless every spring,
leaf, stalk and frond.
Bless the spotted egg,
splashes in a pond.

Bless the stray dog,
the tramp in the road.
Bless twice the poor
and their heavy load.

Dennis Carter

Joe Bright

By day, shut in his workshop,
Joe Bright cuts bits of tin,
And smooths them out and flattens them
Until they're paper thin.

At dusk Joe Bright flies skywards
With boxes, bags and jars,
And on the branches of the dark
He hangs a million stars.

Richard Edwards

Night-spell

Close your eyes
    and wish for light
to chase away
    the net of night.

The stars are only
    down the street,
and deep in sleep
    it's there we'll meet.

Rest your head
   and dream till dawn,
in sleep be free
   as a fleet-foot fawn.

The stars are only
   down the street,
and deep in sleep
   it's there we'll meet.

Take into sleep
   this night-spell charm
to set you safe
   against all harm.

The stars are only
   down the street,
and deep in sleep
   it's there we'll meet.

John Rice

Diamond Poem – Dawn

Light
Seeps out
From dark sky,
Creeps over fields
Of glistening dew,
Wakening birds
Who chorus:
Day is
Born:

John Foster

New Day

The day is so new
You can hear it yawning,
Listen:

The new day
is yawning
and stretching

and waiting to start.

In the clear blue sky
I hear the new day's heart.

Ian McMillan

This Is the Day

This is the sort of day
I should like to wrap
In shiny silver paper
And only open when it's raining,

This is the sort of day
I should like to hide
In a secret drawer to which
Only I have the key,

This is the sort of day
I should like to hang
At the back of the wardrobe
To keep me warm when winter comes,

This is the day
I should like to last forever,

This is my birthday.

June Crebbin

Inside the Morning

Inside the morning is a bird,
Inside the bird is a song,
Inside the song is a longing,

And the longing is to fill the morning.

June Crebbin

Leaf Lines

As I look at
this autumn leaf,
fallen from its tree,
I see how it has
ribs and flesh
like you and me.

Tony Mitton

What Is Fog?

Puffs of dragon smoke
Curling round hedges and trees.

Clouds of steam from a giant's kettle
Pouring out over the city.

The breath from a dinosaur's nostrils
Blurring the world into a grey shadow.

John Foster

The Music of the Wind

The wind makes **LOUD** music.
It roars above the rooftops,
it drums beneath the floor,
it howls around the gable-end
and rat-a-tats the door.

The wind makes *quiet* music.
It whistles down the chimney,
it tiptoes through a tree,
it hums against the window-pane
and whispers tunes to me.

Wes Magee

Windy Nights

Whenever the moon and the stars are set,
   Whenever the wind is high,
All night long in the dark and wet,
   A man goes riding by.
Late in the night when the fires are out,
Why does he gallop and gallop about?

Whenever the trees are crying aloud,
   And ships are tossed at sea,
By, on the highway, low and loud,
   By at the gallop goes he.
By at the gallop he goes, and then
By he comes back at the gallop again.

Robert Louis Stevenson

A Ragged Band

The wind at night's
a tin can kicked round by a team of ghostly children,
an ocean wave roaring one end of the street to the other,
a skeleton's teeth chattering with cold,
a scarecrow's nightmare,
a drunken herd of elephants,
a bag of bones clattering around the yard,
a line of trees dancing an Irish jig!

It's
a moon-scolding cat,
an out-of-sorts drummer,
a gang of ghosts out for a bone-rattle,
a squall of hissing snakes,
a vicious kitten clawing the house fronts,
a thief testing all the windows,
the End Of All Time Orchestra!

Brian Morse

Snowed In

The house wears a muffler.
The road outside is still.
The postman hasn't called.
His van can't climb the hill.

The puddles are polished
and powdered in snow;
the trees dressed in white
for the Christmas card show.

Pie Corbett

Seasons of Trees

In spring
The trees
Are a beautiful sight
Dressed in blossom
Pink and white.

In summer
The trees
Are full of treats
Apples and pears
And cherries to eat.

In autumn
The trees
Are red and gold
And the leaves fall down
As the days grow cold.

In winter
The trees
Are bare and plain
Waiting for spring
To dress them again.

Julie Holder

Johnny Come over the Water

Johnny come over the water
And make the sun shine through.
Johnny come over the water
And paint the sky with blue.

Cover the field and the meadow
With flowers of red and gold,
And cover with leaves the simple trees
That stand so bare and cold.

Johnny come over the water,
Turn the white grass to hay.
It's winter, winter all the year
Since you went away.

Charles Causley

Winter Walk

Walking home from Granny's
On a dark and snowy night,
Everything looks ghostly
In the shadowy street light.

All is still and quiet.
No footsteps can be heard,
Except the crunch beneath us.
Too cold to say a word.

Wendy Larmont

Coming out of Hibernation

Black bats hang in barns,
Their wings folded
Like old umbrellas.

Snoring hedgehogs sleep
Curled up tight,
Like hairbrushes
Beneath crisp leaves.

Grey squirrels dream in dreys
Of scrambled twigs.

Toads squat,
Their eyelids drawn down.
As still as stones
Tucked beneath
The compost heap.

Sly spring sunlight
Creeps through clouds;
Bulbs break the warm earth
And the world wears
A new coat.

Bats unfurl their creased wings
And blink their way
From hollow tree stumps.

Hedgehogs uncurl
And sniff, sipping the sunlight.

The blotched toad
Gulps in warm air –
He puffs his wrinkled cheeks
Like an old man.

The squirrel arches her back
And tests a branch;
Before running
Like a rat
To find her acorn stash.

The world rolls onto its side
And stretches out its legs.
Reaching for its sunglasses,
It rubs its earthy hands.

The spring sings out loud.

Pie Corbett

It's Spring

It's spring
And the garden is changing its clothes,
Putting away
Its dark winter suits,
Its dull scarves
And drab brown overcoats.

Now, it wraps itself in green shoots,
Slips on blouses
Sleeved with pink and white blossom,
Pulls on skirts of daffodil and primrose,
Snowdrop socks and purple crocus shoes,
Then dances in the sunlight.

John Foster

The Wind and the Sun

Said the wind to the sun, 'I can carry off kites
And howl down the chimney on blustery nights.
I can sail boats and set windmills in motion,
Rattle the windows and ruffle the ocean.'

And the old sun grinned
At the wild winter wind.

250

Said the sun to the wind, 'I turn night into day,
Ice into water and grass into hay.
I can melt puddles and open up roses.
I can paint rainbows, and freckles on noses.'

And the old sun grinned
At the wild winter wind.

Said the wind to the sun, 'You'll be sorry you spoke.
Down on the road is a man with a cloak.
If you're so clever then let's see you prove it.
We'll take it in turns to see who can remove it.'

And the old sun grinned
At the wild winter wind.

The wind blew the trees till the boughs bent and broke.
He bowled the man's hat off and howled round his cloak.
He blew and he blustered, he tossed and he tugged it.
The man wrapped it round him and tightly he hugged it.

And the old sun grinned
At the wild winter wind.

'Take a rest,' said the sun. 'Let me shine on him now.'
He shone till the man started mopping his brow.
The man settled down in the shade of some boulders.
He undid his cloak and it slipped from his shoulders.

And the old sun grinned
At the wild winter wind.

Julia Donaldson

What Is the Sun?

the Sun is an orange dinghy
   sailing across a calm sea

it is a gold coin
   dropped down a drain in Heaven

the Sun is a yellow beach ball
   kicked high into the summer sky

it is a red thumbprint
   on a sheet of pale blue paper

the Sun is a milk bottle's gold top
   floating in a puddle.

Wes Magee

Ice Lolly

Red rocket
on a stick.
If it shines,
lick it quick.

Round the edges,
on the top,
round the bottom,
do not stop.

Suck the lolly.
Lick your lips.
Lick the sides
as it drips

off the stick –
quick, quick,
lick, lick –
Red rocket
on a stick.

Pie Corbett

Sea Shore

Sandy shore and seaweed;
Rocks and cockleshells;
Pebbles round and salty;
Dead fish smells.

253

Sun on bending water;
Donkeys' jingling bells;
Hoofprints in sand-ripples;
Saltwater wells.

Boats against the sunshine;
Seagulls' squealing hells;
Spray on brown faces;
Small boys' yells.

John Kitching

City River

wall-slapper
    factory-passer
        rubbish-receiver
            backstreet-winder
                bridge-nudger
           steps-licker
        park-wanderer
     summer-shiner
        ducks-supporter
           choppy-water
              crowd-delighter
                onward-traveller

June Crebbin

My Father Gave Me Seeds

My father gave me seeds.
I gave the seeds to the earth.
The earth gave me flowers.
I gave the flowers to the bees.
The bees gave me honey.
I gave the honey to a merchant.
The merchant gave me cloth.
I gave the cloth to a tailor.
The tailor gave me a cloak.
I gave the cloak to a farmer.
The farmer gave me seeds.
I gave the seeds to my father.
My father gave thanks for the seeds.

John Foster

A tree

A tree
is not like you and
me – it waits around quite
patiently – catching kites and
dropping leaves – reaching out to touch
the breeze . . . A tree all day will stand and stare
clothed in summer, winter: bare – it has no shame
or modesty . . . A tree's generosity is the greatest in the
world – it gives a home to every bird, every squirrel,
feeds them too – to every dog it is a loo . . . And after dark
what does it do? Catch a falling star or two? Shimmy in the
old moonlight? Or maybe have a conker fight? A tree can
give an awful lot: the wood to make a baby's cot – pencils,
paper, tables, chairs – lolly sticks as well as stairs . . . And
that's not it, there's more you know – a tree, you see, it
likes to grow those fancy fruits and nibbly nuts –
lots of lovely snacks for us! Without a tree
we could not live – a tree, it seems
just loves to give –
but us:
we
chop
we
take
we
burn
that's
what we
do in return

James Carter

Answers to Riddles

Answer to *Humpty-Dumpty*

- egg

Answer to *As I Went over Lincoln Bridge*

- hedgehog

Answers to *Four Riddles*

- hair
- teeth
- a finger
- fog

Answer to *Guess What I Am*

- an owl

Glossary of Terms

Acrostic
This is a poetic form that uses the initial letters of a key word at the beginning of each line, e.g.

Creeps through the darkness,
Along the garden wall,
Tail swaying.

You can also hide the key word within the poem, e.g.

Animal Riddle
       Like a small Bear
              bundles over the dark road,
      brushes pAst the front gate,
          as if she owns the joint,
     rolls the Dustbin,
           like an expert barrel rider,
tucks into yesterday's Garbage,
            crunches worms for titbits,
   wakes us from dEep sleep,
           blinks back at torchlight,
  our midnight feasteR,
        ghost-friend,
        moon-lit,
         zebra bear.

Pie Corbett

Action Verse
These are rhymes that involve an action. They are usually performed by small children!

Adjective
A word that is added or linked to a noun to describe it.
e.g. the *red* dress.

Adverb
A word which adds to a verb (how, where or when). Many end in 'ly'.
e.g. she ran *quickly*.

Alliteration
This is when poets use the same sound close by.
e.g. *the cruel cat cautiously crept by*.
Alliteration is very useful because it draws the reader's attention to the words. It makes the words memorable – often advertisers use alliteration for this reason (Buy a *Ticktock* today). You can have great fun with alliterative sentences by creating Tongue-Twisters. You may know this one:
She sells seashells on the seashore.

Alphabet Poem
This is a poem written using the letters of the alphabet, e.g.
A is an ant,
B is a baboon . . .

Ballad

This is a formal poem or song that is meant to be performed aloud. Ballads tell stories, using a regular pattern, usually with verses and a chorus, e.g.

'O Mary, go and call the cattle home,
  And call the cattle home,
  And call the cattle home,
  Across the sands of Dee!'
The western wind was wild and dank with foam,
  And all alone went she.

From 'The Sands of Dee' by Charles Kingsley.

Calligram

This is a picture poem made of letters representing an aspect of the poem. For instance, if the word chosen was 'shake' the writer might write the word using a wobbly typeface: 's h a k e'. In the example below the words are leaning across to reflect the meaning.
The sloping wall.

Chant

This is a rhyme that has a strong beat and rhythm. It can be chanted aloud to good effect.

Choral Poem

A poem for speaking aloud by a whole group.

Cinquain
This was invented by the American poet Adelaide Crapsey
– it is rather like a haiku – consisting of five lines, using
twenty-two syllables, arranged in a sequence 2, 4, 6, 8, 2.
The last line is often a surprise.

Classic Poem
This is a poem that has stood the test of time. Its author
may be dead but the poem is considered to be sufficiently
memorable still to be printed and read.

Cliché
This is an overused, stale phrase or word combination.
e.g. the cotton-wool clouds.

Collage Poem
This is a list poem, where each line adds a new image.
Many writers use this technique, e.g.

I remember the waves rushing up the beach.
I remember the gulls dipping over the headland.
I remember the black, jagged rocks . . .

Concrete Poem
This is a sort of shape poem where the design of the words
adds extra meaning to the poem; it relies on the layout of
the words for full impact. The Scottish poet Ian Hamilton
Finlay literally made poems out of stone and put them in
his garden!

Conversation
This is a poem written as if there was a conversation taking place. Often good for performing aloud!

Counting Rhyme
Rhymes that use numbers,
e.g. One, two, buckle my shoe . . .

Couplet
Two consecutive, paired lines of poetry, e.g.

Nor I half turn to go yet turning stay,
Remember me when no more day by day

Determiner
A word that tells you more about a noun, e.g.

A dog
Each dog
Every dog
The dog

Duologue
A conversation poem between two parties.

Eye (or Sight) Rhyme
These are words that look as if they might rhyme but do not, e.g. cough/through.

Figurative Language
Use of metaphor or simile to create an impression or mood. Figurative language helps to build up a picture in the reader's mind. Poets use it all the time!

Free Verse
Poetry not constrained by metrical or rhyming patterns. (Some would say that sometimes free verse is just an excuse for not working hard at creating a form!)

Haiku
This is a very popular Japanese form of poetry. It is brief, related to the seasons/nature, expresses a sense of awe or insight, written using concrete sense images and not abstractions, in the present tense. It is often written as three lines, of seventeen syllables arranged in a sequence 5, 7, 5, though not necessarily. A verbal snapshot, capturing the essence of a moment/scene. Some haiku are only a line or two. The idea is to paint a word-picture, e.g.

Flies stalk the cup's rim
Washing their hands, fidgeting
In the sullen heat.

Half-rhyme
These are words which almost rhyme.
e.g. grip/grab.

Homograph
A word with the same spelling as another, but a different meaning.
e.g. the *calf* was eating/my *calf* was aching.

Idiom
A phrase often used that is not meant literally. Its meaning is understood by the people who use it, but cannot be inferred from knowledge of the individual words. e.g. over the moon, under the weather, thick as two short planks.

Imagery
This is when you are using language to create a vivid sensory image or picture in the reader's mind. This is done with similes and metaphors but also by carefully selecting the right word.

Internal Rhyme
This is when the poet puts rhymes within lines, e.g.
Lizard cars cruise by.
Their radiators *grin*.
Thin headlights stare . . .

Kenning
This is a sort of riddle. It was used in Old English and Norse poetry to name something without using its name, e.g. mouse catcher (cat). The Anglo Saxons named their swords in this way, e.g. bone cruncher.

List Poem

This is a poem that is written rather like a list, using the same repeating phrase to introduce each idea, e.g.

I saw a fish on fire.
I saw a bird swim in oil.
I saw . . .

Metaphor

Metaphors are rather like similes, except in a simile you say that one thing is like another. In a metaphor you just say that one thing IS another – so you are writing about something as if it was something else. 'The moon is like a smile' is a simile. 'The moon is a smile' or 'the moon smiles' are metaphors.

Metre

This is the term used to describe the organization of poetry by the pattern of regular rhythm.

Monologue

This is when a character speaks aloud. Monologues are found in plays but some poems are written to be spoken aloud by a character.

Narrative Poem

This is quite simply a story poem. Ballads are a form of narrative poem.

Nonsense Poem

This is poetry that uses nonsense words ('Twas Brillig and the slithy toves) or writes about nonsensical events (We put on our pigeons and swam through the custard).

Noun

A noun is the name of a thing, person, place or idea.

Nursery Rhyme

This is a rhyme that parents sing to very small children.

Onomatopoeia

These are words that sound like their meaning.
e.g. the busy bee buzzes.

Oral Poem

This is a poem that has been passed down through the generations by word of mouth

Performance Poem

This is a poem intended for performance. Often direct and lively, using rhythm and rhyme. Great fun to join in with. Of course, most poems can be performed!

Personification

This is a form of metaphor and great fun to write. It is when you take an object and pretend it has come alive – rather like sprinkling Disney dust on to broomsticks so that they get up and start dancing, e.g.

The wind moaned.
The trees stooped down.
The bushes whispered.

Playground Chant/Rhyme
This is a rhyme that children tell in the playground. It is often used for skipping, clapping, ball-bouncing games, ring games and dipping.

Powerful Verb
A powerful verb draws the attention of the reader to the action. It brings energy to the writing by being more extreme and descriptive, e.g.

'Get out!' she *screamed.*

Prayer
Words spoken to a god.

Pun
This is a play on words, where a word has two meanings. e.g. the book is not red/the book is not read.

Rap
This is a lively form of poetry that uses strong rhythm and rapid pace. It is often performed with music and is rather like rapid, rhyming speech.

Refrain
This is a repeated chorus.

Rhyme

These are words that make the same end sounds, e.g. dig/fig. Half-rhymes are words that almost rhyme, e.g. slip/sleep. End rhymes fall at the end of the lines in poetry. Internal rhymes come in the middle of the lines. Eye rhymes look as if they should rhyme but do not, e.g. cough/through.

Rhythm

Poems should have rhythm so that the poem is memorable. Rhythm is the more or less regular alternation of light and heavy beats in speech or music to provide a beat.

Riddle

A form of poetry where the subject is hidden and the reader has to guess what is being written about.

Shape Poem

This is a poem that is written in a shape. The shape usually reflects the subject of the poem.

Simile

Similes are used a lot by poets. A simile is when you are saying that one thing is like another, to create a picture in the reader's mind. There are two sorts of simile:
1. Using 'like', e.g. a saddle *like* a mushroom.
2. Using 'as', e.g. as slow *as* grass growing.

Song
Words that are intended to be accompanied by music.
They often have several verses with a repeated chorus in
between.

Surrealism
This is a form of writing that is rather crazy and dream-
like – where all sorts of impossible things happen.

Syllable
Each beat in a word is a syllable.
e.g. *cat* has one syllable but *kitten* has two (kit-ten).

Synonym
Words which have the same, or very similar, meaning, e.g.
wet/damp. Avoids overuse of any word; adds variety.

Thin Poem
A shape poem written down or across the page with only a
few letters or words per line so that it is thin!

Tongue-twister
These are short lines which alliterate or rhyme. They are
often very hard to say, especially when repeated quickly,
e.g. unique, New York.

Traditional Rhyme
This is a rhyme that has been known for many years.
Many of them are nursery rhymes.

Verb
A word or group of words which names an action or state of being. A Doing Word.

Word Puzzle
A range of word games, often in poetic form.

A–Z of Advice for Young Poets

Audience – present poems by performing, making posters, post-its, use email or stick them in a bottle and let them float away.

Brainstorm – look or think about your subject – make lists of words and ideas to use in your poems.

Concentrate – learn to look carefully.

Decide – writing is about choosing words and ideas. Read your work aloud to see and hear how it sounds. Listen to your own writing as if you had never heard it before.

Experiment – try out different words and combinations.

Feelings – write about what moves you.

Grow – let poems have time to grow. Come back to them after a while and see how they sound!

Habit – keep on practising; write every day.

Imagine – take what you know and invent a bit; play 'what if . . .' or 'supposing'. Cars could break-dance and telegraph poles tickle you under the chin.

Juggle – keep throwing the words up into the air, testing them out.

Know – write about what you know about – your interests and obsessions.

Look – become a close observer of the world.

Mimic – borrow patterns from other poets. Read daily and learn good poems – let beautiful language live forever in your mind.

Notebook – keep a notebook to jot down observations, ideas, and words, things people say, funny things, rhythms and . . . wrestle with words.

Opposites – try words and ideas that do not go together – 'loud silences' and 'soft granite'.

Play – play with ideas, so that in the window you see a sunflower blossom, so that the moon grins and the sun is a giant gobstopper.

Question – ask tigers who made them and why the stars are so silent. Then reply.

Recreate – use words to capture your experience. Try to write down what things are really like.

Secrets – use your imagination to discover the secret world – of stones and snakes . . .

Trim – avoid using too many words – just choose the best ones.

Unique – find your own ideas.

Voice/s – try writing as if you were a creature, an object or someone else, write in role – and give the world a voice.

Word hoard – get in the habit of collecting and tasting the flavour of words.

X-ray – look so hard that you can see to the heart.

Yourself – put yourself into your poems as well as the subject.

Zeal – write with energy, enjoyment and celebration.

A–Z of Poetry-reading Ideas

Assembly – hold a poetry assembly where each class performs poems.

Buy words – which words would you buy or borrow from a poem? Make a class list of tasty words.

Cut up and close reading – cut up a poem for someone else to put together – by word, line or verse. Or cut out words and leave spaces to be filled.

Drawing – illustrate a poem – create poem posters.

Enthusiasm – discuss what you liked in a poem, what you didn't like – draw up a desert island list of top ten poems or poets. Hold a vote across the school.

Feelings – read and discuss what poems make you feel and think. Write down or share your first thoughts.

Gossip – chat about poets and poems. Hold regular 'recommendation' sessions where you read aloud a poem that you think others will enjoy.

Highlights – which are the highlights of a poem? Which is a poet's best poem and why? Use a highlighter to identify favourite words or lines.

Imitate – copy patterns and write a poem yourself.

Journals – keep a poetry journal – each week stick in a new poem that you like.

Know it by heart – learn poems by heart. Chant, perform and sing poems out loud.

Letters – write to poets . . . or to characters in their poems.

Memories – what memories does a poem stir? What do you see in your mind and what does it remind you of?

Newspaper headlines – create a newspaper headline and article about a poem or what is happening in a poem, especially narrative poetry.

Organize – a poetry reading or poetry day. Invite poets into school for book weeks or arts festivals.

Performance – perform poems – make tapes and videos. Send these to other classes or schools.

Question – ask questions about poems – what puzzles you? What are you not certain about? Discuss mysteries. Remember: not everything makes sensible sense – sometimes poems have to be experienced and not just understood.

Reread – keep rereading a poem to let its meaning creep upon you – and to let the words sink forever into your mind.

Swap – swap poems over. Find one you think your partner would enjoy.

Title – hide the title of a poem – what might the poem be called?

Underline – use a coloured pencil to underline, star or circle parts of a poem that are of interest – likes, dislikes, puzzles or patterns.

Video – video a reading or class performance of a poem. Put on a poetry show.

Weekly – have a poet of the week or month – read their poems each day.

X-ray – put on your X-ray vision when reading – try to see and listen to the heart of a poem.

Yardstick – collect a few poems that act as your poetic yardstick – what is a really good poem by which all others have to be judged? Which are the great ones . . . and why?

Zodiac – create a zodiac of poems – one for each star sign (or month).

Instructions for Circle Games,
Action and Playground Rhymes

Many teachers invent their own actions to different rhymes – and, of course, children will also add in actions and change words if encouraged, thereby making the rhymes their own. Most of the rhymes have many different versions. I am lucky enough to have played many of these games when I was younger, as well as having taught them to children in schools. Some I picked up from teachers and many from children in my visits to schools over the last thirty years. For skipping, clapping and dipping rhymes it may be worth asking older children to teach the younger ones their way of doing it. Anyway, here are some suggestions.

Pat-a-cake – the basic clapping pattern

This is probably the first clapping rhyme that children ever meet. Use a simple clapping pattern in pairs. You may need to show the children how to do this – and for some children it takes quite a lot of practice. The main clapping pattern that accompanies many rhymes is as follows:

- Clap your own hands together
- Then clap your right hand to your partner's right hand
- Clap your own hands together again
- Then clap your left hand to your partner's left hand
- Clap your own hands together

- (Sometimes you then clap both hands with your partner)

Keep this pattern going in time to the rhythm of the rhyme.

Circle Songs

The Mulberry Bush

This is the simplest of circle songs. Stand in a circle and join hands. Sing and dance round. Stop on the verses, '*This is the way we . . .*' and add in appropriate actions, e.g. pretending to scrub floors. Of course, you can add in extra verses such as '*. . . clean our teeth*', '*. . . wash our hands*', etc.

Ring-a-ring o' Roses

When I used to play this game we stood in a circle and danced round as we sang. We stopped, pretended to sneeze and then fell down! Legend has it that this song is about the plague . . . though there is no evidence for this at all! It is more likely that the rhyme has its origins in Maytime celebrations, with the rose as a symbolic gift between loved ones.

Down in the Valley

Make a circle and use a dipping rhyme to choose one person, who stands in the middle. Circle round, singing the first verse, putting the name of the selected person into line 3. This person then chooses someone to come into the middle, and they pretend to have tea while the second verse is being sung.

The Farmer's in His Den

This has to be the most popular ring game. We had various versions of this. Choose a farmer to go in the middle – the farmer chooses a wife, the wife chooses a child, and so on. The best bit is at the end, when everyone comes in to pat the bone. If this gets out of hand, then the farmer alone pats the bone. The bone becomes the farmer the next time. A more elaborate version is to have those in the middle form a second circle and both circles move round, while singing, in opposite directions. Originally the 'den' was probably a 'dell', meaning a copse.

Oats and Beans and Barley Grow

Everyone forms a circle, skipping round and singing the song. A farmer takes a turn in the centre, acting out sowing seeds, taking ease, stamping, clapping, etc. The wife is chosen and the two can spin round in the middle or act out the last part. This may have begun life as some sort of symbolic wedding or spring fertility chant.

Rosy Apple

There are lots of ways to perform this rhyme. One way is for the pair to form a simple arch and everyone else passes under the bridge until the last part, when the arms descend and whoever is trapped becomes the next bride or groom.

Let's Go to Kentucky

This is a lovely one to sing as it gallops along at a good pace! The circle dances round the 'senorita', who stands in the middle – she 'shakes it' (wiggling and wobbling), 'rumbles' (side to side) and then spins round.

There Was a Princess Long Ago

This one has to be as well known as 'The Farmer's in His Den'. Move round the circle, singing. Select a princess, fairy and prince. The princess stands in the middle. Now act out each verse, e.g. lift hands for the *'big high tower'*, fairy waves wand, princess curls up asleep, circle all wave hands for trees, prince trots round, chops trees, wakes princess – and at the end everyone skips round.

Poor Jenny

This rather sad song is also popular. One child acts as Jenny while everyone else moves round. She acts each verse and – if brave enough – sings verse 3 solo. She also chooses a 'loved one' – usually to much hilarity and squealing!

Brown Girl in the Ring

This song was made popular by Boney M. some years ago. Hold hands in a circle and chant the song, moving joined hands up and down. The person in the middle pretends to skip, wriggles to show the 'motion' (or 'emotion', as we sang), chooses a partner and whirls them round.

Banyan Tree

There are different ways to play this game. Form a circle in pairs (girl/boy) and act the rhyme out, complete with bowing, joining hands and promenading round in a circle.

Do You Know the Muffin Man?

My best version of this is to have a static circle. The circle sings verse 1. The person in the middle is blindfolded and moves round till verse 2. They point to someone and sing verse 2. Then he or she has to guess who they think it is – to help, the person pointed to may have to say, 'I am the muffin man,' in a disguised voice.

Pop Goes the Weasel!

We used to sing the first verse just for the fun of the sound of the words. Then at school we had to play this in PE. We formed lots of small circles. Each circle has a weasel in the middle and one person is the weasel who runs outside a ring. Everyone skips round till you get to '*Pop goes the weasel*'.

The weasels then have to dash into a new ring, leaving the last child to get there outside.

Nuts in May

This sounds like another spring celebration. Split the children into two groups, who stand facing each other. One line skips towards the other, singing the first verse. The second group stands still until the second verse, when they sing and skip towards the first line. The first team then sings the third verse, naming whom they nominate. The other group does the same. The chosen pair then stands in the middle for a tug-of-war. The loser has to join the other side.

In and Out the Windows

There are quite a few games in which the children use the same dance pattern – known often as 'in and out the windows'. Form a circle, holding hands high to form a series of arches. One boy dances in and out of the arches, round the ring, while verse 1 is sung. The boy stands beside a chosen girl for verse 2. In verse 3 they both thread in and out the windows with the boy chasing the girl – in the final verse they go into the middle and shake hands . . . Though in my day you tried to kiss the girl!

Dusty Bluebells

I misheard the name of this game and we all called it 'Dusky Bluebells'! This is more popular nowadays because you do not need a boy to chase a girl! Make a circle of arches as in 'In and Out the Windows'. One person is chosen to weave round while verse 1 is sung. Wherever the player stops, he or she taps the shoulder of the person in front of them as the second verse is sung. The song returns to the beginning, but now both players dance round – in this way you keep going till everyone is weaving round an invisible circle!

Lou, Lou, Skip to Me Lou

For this one you can have a static circle. A chosen pair skips round the circle during verse 1. The partner rejoins the circle and the person left has to skip round during verse 2. Another partner is chosen and off they skip for verse 3.

The Big Ship Sails on the Alley, Alley O

This one has a wonderful tune for singing. Stand in a line, holding hands. The person at one end puts his or her hand against a wall, forming an arch – it helps if this is someone quite tall! The person at the other end of the line leads everyone under the arch as the first verse is sung. The person at the end of the line is tugged round so that his/her arms are crossed. The player next to him/her forms a new arch and the circle spins round again and under his arch. If you keep going, you end up with a circle of people with their arms crossed and as a circle they sing the final verses, bobbing their heads up and down. We used to change 'September' to November or December, depending on how we felt!

One Little Elephant

This used to be popular with the infants in my school; I think it was because of the idea of an elephant on a spider's web. Form a static circle. The 'elephant' plods round the outside as the first verse is sung, swinging an arm as a trunk. The elephant taps someone on the shoulder, who joins on with his or her trunk. Keep going till everyone is trooping round an invisible circle.

The Hokey Cokey

This used to be the staple diet of many a party when I was younger. Form a circle and follow the actions – on the chorus everyone joins hands and rushes into the middle and back out again.

The Grand Old Duke of York

We used to march up and down to this nursery rhyme when I first went to school. Form two lines, with a couple who march down the middle and back. They cast off and everyone follows them round till they form an arch for the rest to pass through.

Drunken Sailor

I learned this when I joined the Cubs – along with games like 'British Bulldog'. You stand in a circle and act out each verse. We made up our own verses, describing what we would do to the drunken sailor, e.g. 'throw him in the sea with his trousers off!!'

How Many Miles to Babylon?

My dad used to sing this to us in a rather slow chant. I imagined Babylon as a distant and magical place. It always worried me that the candle might blow out! Form a long line, holding hands – the players at either end of the line say the lines in turn as questions and answers. On the request to 'open your gates', the two players at the other end hold their hands high to make an arch and the players pass through. The 'arch' ends up twisted round with their arms folded. Eventually everyone is joined in this way, rather like a stitch woven into a cloth. This is known as 'threading the needle'.

The Bells of London

This is another song that we played at school. Two players form an arch. Everyone passes through the arch as the song is sung. At the end of the song you sing:

Here comes a candle to light you to bed
Here comes a chopper to chop off your head
Chip chop chip chop
The last man's DEAD.

On the word 'dead', the person passing through is captured. This person then has to say if they are an orange or a lemon.

You keep going till everyone has been captured. Then you form two teams, oranges and lemons, for a tug of war!

London Bridge Is Falling Down

This is played in the same way as 'The Bells of London'. You can make up new verses by changing the words, e.g. '*Build it up with ham and eggs*', etc. On 'my fair lady' you capture someone, and to decide which side to join, and then they stand behind the relevant player's back. The game ends with a tug of war!

Action Rhymes and Songs

Peter Works with One Hammer

We used to sing this as a simple counting rhyme. You beat in time to the song, raising a finger for each hammer. Some people use a fist for hammers one and two, then feet for the third and fourth hammer . . . and the fifth hammer is the head – but that always made me feel sick!

I'm a Little Teapot

This has to be the most popular action rhyme ever. Stand up to sing the song, pretending to be a teapot, shouting out the last line!

Miss Polly Had a Dolly

There are lots of ways to sing this song. Everyone can sing, and a few children can act it out. You can clap hands with a partner in time to the song, patting each other's hands forcefully on the repeated words, e.g. 'sick, sick, sick'.

When Susie Was a Baby

This is still a popular rhyme, and has various dodgy versions! It can be an action rhyme, where you act out each verse, e.g. thumb in mouth, skipping, hands in the air, pretend to kiss, rock the baby, knit, and die, moaning and ending by freezing on the spot. Some children clap the first line of each verse.

If You're Happy and You Know It

Stand in a circle and sing with gusto. Follow the instructions, keeping in time. This song just makes you feel happy!

The Wheels on the Bus

This is another very popular action song which children and teachers adapt. For each verse, invent actions and vary the volume, for instance by shouting 'too much noise' or whispering 'fall fast asleep'.

This Old Man

This is a good counting rhyme with a great tune. For each number, hold up the relevant number of fingers and then invent actions for each verse, e.g. pretend to beat a drum, tap the shoe, tap your knee, etc.

Old Macdonald Had a Farm

This song is very popular because of the sound effects for different animals. Add in all the common farm animals and then experiment with wild animals.

Five Little Speckled Frogs

This song has a most attractive tune. It is another good counting song. Create actions, e.g. hold up the right number of fingers, sit the fingers on your other hand (the log), rub tummy for 'yum, yum', pretend to dive into the pool and make a swimming action.

I Have a Dog

This is another one where you can make up actions and words for how Rags the dog moves, e.g. flip-flop – hands flap like ears; wig-wag – wriggle side to side; zig-zag – flick hands in zigzag shape.

Little Rabbit Foo Foo

In some versions, the field mice get 'bopped' upon the head. Form a circle. Choose two players to be the rabbit and the fairy. They stand in the middle and act out the song. The fairy keeps giving chances to Foo Foo until in the end she turns Foo Foo into something, e.g. a toad, an alien . . .

I Had a Little Monkey

This verse was always popular with children in my school. Everyone chants the rhyme and some children act out what happens. The lady with the alligator purse acts 'posh', with plenty of bottom wiggling for fun! In some daring versions, the verdict is 'he's got wind' . . .

Old Roger

This one has a rather slow tune that must have come out of the folksong tradition. It can be played by standing in a circle, and Roger starts by lying in the centre. The verses are acted out and the old woman becomes Roger for the next time. An interesting aspect of this rhyme is that in some traditional tales from different parts of the world a dead person becomes a plant – a juniper tree or bush. So perhaps we cannot blame Roger's ghost for getting cross when the old woman starts to pick up parts of his body!

A Frog He Would a-Wooing Go

We used to sing 'a froggie went a-wooing' and I loved the line 'with a rowley, powley, gammon and spinach'. You can perform this by standing in a circle, with the actors acting out the verses and singing their parts.

Soldier, Soldier, Will You Marry Me?

Use dressing-up clothes to play this one. Someone is the soldier and someone else is the pretty maid who has to dress the soldier up.

Old Noah's Ark

This can be sung as a counting rhyme, showing the right number of fingers each time. Of course, you could go the whole hog and use masks for the animals and perform it at an assembly . . .

There Was an Old Lady

This is another one that can be performed using masks, with the class singing the song in the background.

Playground rhymes

Dipping Rhymes

Use these to choose players or for taking turns.

Skipping Rhymes

I Like Silver

In my school the children used to sing a different version of this: 'I like coffee, I like tea, I like *[insert name here]* in with me'. The person who is singing and skipping names a friend, who joins the skipper and they skip as a pair.

Bumper Car

This is a very popular skipping rhyme. Two people turn a long rope. Someone skips in and, on 'whizzed round the corner', jumps out and runs round to jump in again. On 'slammed on the brakes', the skipper traps the rope between the legs. They then start skipping and everyone counts – the skipper who manages the highest number wins.

Blue Bells, Cockle Shells

This is a classic skipping rhyme using a long rope – everyone takes it in turn to see who can do the most skips.

Early in the Morning

Play this like 'Blue Bells, Cockle Shells' to see how many letters arrive and then chant the alphabet. Whatever letter a mistake is made upon, the skipper names someone.

I'm a Girl Scout

This one also uses a long rope. The skipper has to perform the actions (salute, bow, spin round) while skipping, and then see who can skip for the most turns of the rope.

Underneath the Apple Tree

This is popular because it determines your future. Use a long rope and someone keeps skipping. You can invent categories to discover whom the players will marry, etc.

Teddy Bear

I have seen this performed just with actions as well as as a skipping rhyme. The skipper performs the actions and spells out g-o-o-d-n-i-g-h-t, trying to get to the end without a slip.

I Went to the Animal Fair

A whole line runs in and joins in, one by one. Keep skipping and singing, losing players as they make mistakes, till only one person is left.

Not Last Night

This can be played like 'Teddy Bear' – the skipper performing actions whilst skipping. Invent more verses so the Spanish lady can salute to the king, comb her hair, brush her teeth, etc.

Clapping rhymes

Have You Ever

This is not only hard to say but it also adds in the element of trying to work with a partner and clap a pattern. The simplest way to do this is always to start the first word and beat of each verse on the knees and then clap your own hands together, then your partner's, then yours, and so on. Once the children can do this, then try this harder version: start the first word and beat of each verse on the knees and then clap your own hands together; follow this by clapping right hands, then own hands, then left hands – ending on both hands with the last word and beat of each verse.

A Sailor Went to Sea Sea Sea

This can be played as an action rhyme. For instance, salute three times on 'sea', chop hands on 'chop', tap knee on 'knee', etc. When the children can manage this rhythmically, you could move to clapping. This could be made fairly simple by starting on own hands together, then both partner's hands, then back to own hands together. Keep this going till the repeated word, when they should clap each other's hands three times, keeping time. Older children may perform this using horizontal clapping.

Three, Six, Nine

When I was younger I misheard the words and for years sang, 'the street Caroline'! It works quite well if you use a simple pattern: clap your own hands together and then your partner's. Once the children get good at this, then try other patterns, e.g. clap own hands then partner's left, then own, then partner's right, then own, etc.

I'm Popeye the Sailor Man

As a child I knew all sorts of versions of this rhyme! Looking at the rhyme now, it makes me wonder if it might be a useful way of teaching punctuation! You can use the basic clapping pattern with a partner, giving two claps together on 'full stop'. Some children end like this: 'comma comma dash dash stop stop turn around and touch the ground FULL STOP'! Older children often do horizontal clapping for this rhyme.

Dom Dom Malayas

This has to be a clapping rhyme from another part of the world that arrived in playgrounds twenty years or so ago – however, I'm not sure of its origins. It is a circle clapping game. Stand in a circle. One player is chosen to start. This person turns to whoever is standing to their left and claps their right hand against their neighbour's left hand. This person now passes the slap on, each time right hand to left hand, round the ring. The rhyme is chanted as this goes on until you reach the word 'three'. Whoever is being slapped on 'three' is out. Keep going until only two players remain. These two join hands and twist them up and down until 'out'. Whoever has their hand on top now gently strokes the top of their partner's hand as they count 'one, two' – and on 'three' tries to slap – but the other player can withdraw their hand!

I Went to a Chinese Restaurant

There are many version of this song. Keep a simple clapping rhythm with a partner, slapping three times on the repeated words. Then carry out the actions: can can, hoola hoop, twist, bow and curtsy, pretend-kiss and shout WOW!

Jamaican Clap Rhyme

Try a simple partner clap or horizontal clapping.

Let's Get the Rhythm of the Street

This is a very lively action rhyme. The opening can be clapped, starting on the knees and then together, back to the knees and then together till you hold up 'ten' fingers. The rest of the rhyme is chanted with relevant actions: stamping feet, clapping hands, wiggling hips and so forth.

Index of Poem Types by Year Group

Reception

Nursery and Traditional Rhymes to Perform

Index of Poem Types by Year Group

Year 1

Index of Poem Types by Year Group

Riddle

Significant Poets – Poems to Read and Perform

Year 2

Other Forms

Patterned Poems to Perform

Index of Poem Types by Year Group

Index of First Lines

Acknowledgements

The compiler and publisher would like to thank the following for permission to use copyright material:

Jez Alborough, 'A Smile', by permission of the author; Moira Andrew, 'Great-aunt Polly' from *Freaky Families*, Macmillan Children's Books (2001); Gerard Benson, 'What I'd Do for My Best Friend' from *Best Friends*, Macmillan Children's Books (2006); Clare Bevan, 'A Bedtime Rhyme for Young Fairies', 'The Song of the Naughty Fairies', 'Fairy Names', 'The Fairy Alphabet', 'Fairy Letters', 'What Do the Fairies Ride?', 'Ten Fairy Facts', 'A Flutter of Fairies', 'A School Report', 'The Mouse-rider's Rap', 'If You Hear . . .' and 'The Fairy Rule Book' all from *Fairy Poems*, Macmillan Children's Books (2004), 'Ten Things a Real Princess Can Do', 'A Few Frightening Things' and 'What the Sleeping Beauty Dreamed' from *Princess Poems*, Macmillan Children's Books (2005), 'Mermaid School', 'The Mermaid Rap' and 'Shimmer Glimmer' from *Mermaid Poems*, Macmillan Children's Books (2005), all by permission of the author; Valerie Bloom, 'Last Lick', by permission of the author; Tony Bradman, 'I Wish I Was a Pirate', reproduced by permission of The Agency (London) Ltd, © Tony Bradman 1991. All rights reserved and enquiries to The Agency, 24 Pottery Lane, London W11 4LZ; Paul Bright, 'Pies' from *Poems About Food*, Weyland (1999), by permission of the author; Dennis Carter, 'Blessings', by permission of the author; James Carter, 'Happy Poem', 'Inside', 'The Key', 'Show & Tell' and 'A tree', all by permission of the author; Charles Causley, 'Quack! Said the Billy Goat', 'Give Me a House' and 'Johnny Come over the Water' from *Collected Poems*, Macmillan Children's Books (2000), by permission of David Higham Associates on behalf of the estate of the author; Paul Cookson, 'These Are the Hands', by permission of the author; John Cotton, 'Kangaroos', by permission of Peggy Cotton; June Crebbin, 'This Is the Day' and 'City River' from *The Crocodile is Coming*, Walker Books (2005), 'The Dinosaur's Dinner' and 'Inside the Morning', by permission of the author; Jan Dean, 'Grandma' from *Freaky Families*, Macmillan Children's Books (2001); Walter de la Mare, 'The Cupboard' from *The Complete Poems of Walter de la Mare*, by permission of the literary trustees of Walter de la Mare and the Society of Authors as their representative; Peter Dixon, 'Shadow Collector' from *The Colour of my Dreams*, Macmillan Children's Books (1998), 'Moving Away' from *The Penguin in the Fridge*, Macmillan Children's Books (2001), 'You Are' and 'Missing Important Things' from *The Tortoise Had a Mighty Roar*, Macmillan Children's Books (2005); Julia Donaldson, 'Noisy Garden', 'The Crow and the Fox', 'The Stork and the Fox', 'The Tortoise and the Hare', 'The Mouse and the Lion' and 'The Wind

and the Sun' from *Crazy Mayonnaisy Mum*, Macmillan Children's Books (2004);
Gina Douthwaite, 'Milking Time' from *Farm Poems*, OUP (1995), by permission
of the author; **Richard Edwards**, 'Wizard' and 'Monster' from *The Word Party*,
Puffin (1986), 'Shaggy Dogs' and 'Joe Bright' from *Teaching the Parrot*, Faber and
Faber Ltd (1996), all by permission of the author; **John Foster**, 'Sitting in My Bath-
tub' from *You Little Monkey*, OUP (1996), 'Who's Afraid?' from *Ghost Poems*,
OUP (1990), 'What Is Fog?' from *Climb Aboard the Poetry Plane*, OUP (2000),
'It's Spring' from *Standing on the Sidelines*, OUP (1995), 'Bizzy Buzzy Bee', 'Sue
Shore', 'Shaun Short', 'Diamond Poem – Dawn' and 'My Father Gave Me Seeds',
all by permission of the author; **Vivian French**, 'The Bee's Story', by permission of
the author; **Katherine Gallagher**, 'Ollie the Wallaby' from *Wordplay*, BBC
Publishing (1993), by permission of the author; **Jamila Gavin**, 'Mirror Friends', by
permission of the author; **Chrissie Gittins**, 'I Don't Want an Avocado for an Uncle',
by permission of the author; **Mary Green**, 'My Spaceship' from *Space Poems*,
Macmillan Children's Books (2006); **David Harmer**, 'The Really Rocking Rocket
Trip', by permission of the author; **Stewart Henderson**, 'Sounds' from *Who Left
Grandad at the Chipshop?*, Lion Hudson (2000); **Ted Hughes**, 'Cat' and 'Cuckoo',
by permission of Faber and Faber Ltd; **Jenny Joseph**, 'Getting Back Home' from
All the Things I See, Macmillan Children's Books (2000), **Penny Kent**, 'Spooky
House', by permission of the author; **John Kitching**, 'Sea Shore' from *Hi-Ran-Ho!*,
Longman (1971), by permission of the author; **Tony Langham**, 'Postcard', by
permission of the author; **Ian McMillan**, 'New Day', by permission of the author;
Wes Magee, 'The Mystery Space Beasts', 'Holiday Trip . . . in the 21st Century',
'Noises in the Night', 'The Guide Dog's Story', 'Our Cats', 'Gran's Old Diary', 'The
Music of the Wind' and 'What is the Sun?', by permission of the author; **Trevor
Millum**, 'Dick's Dog',by permission of the author; **Tony Mitton**, 'The Cave' and
'Rickety Train Ride' from *Pip*, Scholastic (2001), and 'Leaf Lines', all by
permission of the author; **John Mole**, 'Buzz Buzz' from *Boo to a Goose*, Peterloo
(1987), by permission of the author; **Michaela Morgan**, 'Mrs Sprockett's Strange
Machine', 'A Big Surprise', 'The Day the Zoo Escaped' and 'Big Fat Budgie', all by
permission of the author; **Brian Morse**, 'Paint' and 'A Ragged Band', by permission
of the author; **Brian Moses**, 'Hippopotamus Dancing' from *Hippopotamus
Dancing and Other Poems*, Cambridge University Press (1994), 'Don't Be Such a
Fusspot' from *I Wish I Could Dine with a Porcupine*, Hodder (2000), by
permission of the author; **Grace Nichols**, 'Granny Granny Please Comb My Hair'
and 'I Like to Stay Up', by permission of Curtis Brown Ltd on behalf of the author;
Gareth Owen, 'Samantha Is Sobbing', by permission of the author; **Brian Patten**,
'Squeezes' from *Gargling with Jelly*, Puffin (1985); **Gervase Phinn**, 'Nativity' from
A Wayne in a Manger, Michael Joseph (2005), by permission of the author; **Irene
Rawnsley**, 'Calling Names', by permission of the author; **John Rice**, 'Bears Don't
Like Bananas' from *Bears Don't Like Bananas*, Simon & Schuster (1991) and

Acknowledgements

'Night-spell', both by permission of the author; **Cynthia Rider**, 'The Alien's Sweet Shop' from *Space Poems*, Macmillan Children's Books (2006); **Michael Rosen**, 'Eddie and the Nappy', by permission of the author; **Coral Rumble**, 'Hiding' from *A Year of Rhymes*, Macmillan Children's Books (2002); **Vernon Scannell**, 'Burying Moses', by permission of the author; **Ian Souter**, 'My Dad's Amazing!', by permission of the author; **Roger Stevens**, 'The Alien', by permission of the author; **Celia Warren**, 'Who's Counting?' and 'Going Upstairs' from *Spectacular Schools*, Macmillan Children's Books (2000), 'Lion' from *Hippo Book of Magic Poems*, Scholastic (1997), all by permission of the author; **David Whitehead**, 'I Wannabe a Wallaby' from *Animal Poems*, Scholastic (1998), by permission of the author; **John Whitworth**, 'The Cheer-up Song' and 'I Hated Everyone Today', by permission of the author; **Bernard Young**, 'Spaceship Shop', by permission of the author.

Every effort has been made to trace the copyright holders, but if any have been inadvertently overlooked then the publishers will be pleased to make the necessary arrangement at the first opportunity.

EVERY KIND OF POEM YOU WILL
EVER NEED AT SCHOOL

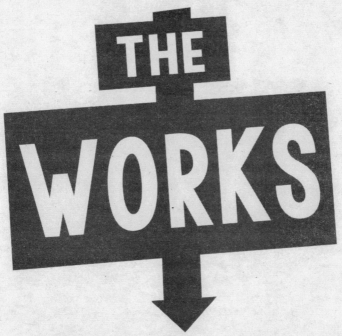

THE
WORKS

CONTAINS A WIDE RANGE OF CONTEMPORARY
AND CLASSIC POEMS AND RHYMES TO
ENJOY, READ, PERFORM AND LEARN BY HEART.
IT IS PACKED WITH BRILLIANT POEMS THAT
WILL DELIGHT ANY READER.

Chosen by
PAUL COOKSON

POEMS ON EVERY SUBJECT AND
FOR EVERY OCCASION

THE
WORKS 2

CONTAINS A WIDE RANGE OF CONTEMPORARY
AND CLASSIC POEMS AND RHYMES TO ENJOY,
READ, PERFORM AND LEARN BY HEART. IT IS A
WELL-CRAFTED ANTHOLOGY WHICH RELATES
LITERACY WORK ACROSS THE CURRICULUM.

Chosen by

BRIAN MOSES and **PIE CORBETT**

POEMS AND RHYMES TO ENJOY, READ, PERFORM AND LEARN BY HEART

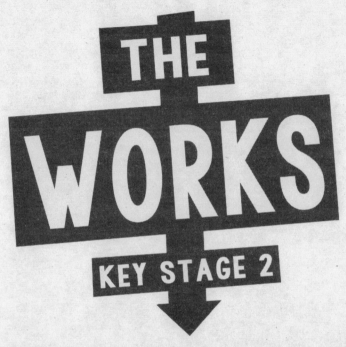

THE WORKS

KEY STAGE 2

CONTAINS A WIDE RANGE OF CONTEMPORARY AND CLASSIC POEMS AND RHYMES TO ENJOY, READ, PERFORM AND LEARN BY HEART – PERFECT FOR CHILDREN IN YEARS 3, 4, 5 AND 6.

Chosen by
PIE CORBETT

Poems by Pie Corbett

Evidence

of

DRAGONS

brings together Pie Corbett's brilliant poems
for the very first time.

The Dragon Whistler

The Dragon Whistler
tucks stars into her pocket,
reaches for a sunset;
purses her moonlit lips
and whistles . . .